W9-AOW-432

UNIVERSITY of MARYLAND
1807
SCHOOL of MEDICINE
200 Years

University of Maryland School of Medicine

The First Two Centuries

1807-2007

1807-2007

University of Maryland School of Medicine

The First Two Centuries

Medical School Milestones ᴔ Faculty Accomplishments ᴔ Alumni Contributions

Larry Pitrof

HISTORIAN
MILFORD M. FOXWELL, JR., M.D. '80

MEDICAL EDITOR
MORTON M. KRIEGER, M.D. '52

MEDICAL ALUMNI ASSOCIATION OF THE UNIVERSITY OF MARYLAND, INC.
BALTIMORE, MARYLAND

Copyright © 2006 by:
The Medical Alumni Association of
the University of Maryland, Inc.
Baltimore, Maryland

All rights reserved

Design: Brushwood Graphics Design Group

Printing: Schmitz Press

Printed in the United States of America

ISBN: 0-9619119-3-X

Contents

❧ *Preface* ❧

Two thousand seven marks the bicentennial celebration of the creation of the University of Maryland School of Medicine, the fifth oldest medical school in the United States. Established in Baltimore as a private medical college in 1807, the institution is recognized today as the founding school of the state's public system of higher education, comprising 11 degree-granting and two research institutions. But it all began with a very determined few.

In the early days of the new Republic, medical doctors struggled to earn public confidence. Training exercises such as cadaver dissection were perceived as ghoulish, and intermittent episodes of violence by the local populace rightly caused medical educators and their pupils to fear for their lives. Despite this opposition, they forged ahead. As a result, medical research has steadily gained legitimacy and respect in the public eye, while American life expectancy has been extended more than 40 years.

This publication traces the 200-year history of our medical school, highlighting accomplishments of our faculty and featuring significant contributions made by many of our 17,000 graduates. The project, sponsored and led by the Medical Alumni Association, continues our efforts to maintain the medical school's rich heritage. We sponsored our first such venture in 1891, with the release of the *Historical Sketch of the University of Maryland School of Medicine (1807–1890)*, written by Eugene F. Cordell, class of 1868. We have him to thank for preserving the early history of our school.

Regarding the collection of information for the most recent 100-plus years, our committee delved into a number of sources listed at the back of this book. Included are the *Bulletin* magazine, the oldest medical alumni magazine in the United States; our annual yearbook *Terrae Mariae Medicus*; and sources maintained in the historical and special collections department of the University of Maryland Baltimore Health Sciences and Human Services Library. We also invited submissions from both faculty and alumni. Drawing information from multiple sources, our committee sought to report pivotal events and individual accomplishments with high accuracy. Nevertheless, we recognize our limitations and apologize for any omissions or errors.

The University of Maryland School of Medicine is a unique and now formidable institution. From its beginning as a modest living room lecture series, our school has evolved into an international leader, advancing biomedical research and providing broad-ranging medical education that nurtures the development of compassionate, inquisitive, ethical and skilled physicians and researchers. It is with great pride that we present this pictorial biography of our school's first 200 years.

Sincerely,

Morton M. Krieger, M.D. '52, *Chair*
Ad-Hoc Bicentennial Book Committee

Richard J. Behles, *Historical Librarian*
Milford M. Foxwell Jr., M.D. '80, *Associate Dean of Admissions*
Sylvan Frieman, M.D. '53
Morton D. Kramer, M.D. '55
Jennifer B. Litchman, *Assistant Dean for Public Affairs*
Larry Pitrof, *Executive Director, Medical Alumni Association*
Jonas R. Rappeport, M.D. '52
Jean Silver-Isenstadt, M.D. '02
Members

Our Medical School

There is a great school, lofty and serene
That stands on the corner of Lombard and Greene
Towering and majestic tis proud of its age
Through many a year it has set the stage
For the passing parade of the medical profession
The time-honored past is its proudest possession

Not that its future is destined to be dim
To express such a thought is an unpardonable sin
For Maryland's history shows it has the basis to be
The best in the nation, both for you and for me
Those circular halls shall never be blighted
Of students' voices and their laughter delighted

The tall graceful columns that guard its halls
Are the symbols that to our mind recalls
The winding stairs leading to the circular rooms
Where the head of Hippocrates solemnly looms
And wisely stares at the collection of men
Gently approves, then relapses to immobility again

~Sidney Sacks, Class of 1946

ANATOMICAL INVESTIGATIONS,

COMPRISING

DESCRIPTIONS OF VARIOUS FASCIÆ

OF THE

HUMAN BODY;

The Discoveries of the Manner in which the Pericardium is formed from the Superficial Fascia; the Capsular Ligament of the Shoulder Joint from the Brachial Fascia; and the Capsular Ligament of the Hip Joint from the Fascia Lata.

TO WHICH IS ADDED

AN ACCOUNT OF SOME IRREGULARITIES OF STRUCTURE

AND

MORBID ANATOMY;

WITH A DESCRIPTION OF A NEW

ANATOMICAL TABLE.

———◆———

BY JOHN D. GODMAN, M. D.

LECTURER ON ANATOMY AND PHYSIOLOGY;

EDITOR OF THE JOURNAL OF FOREIGN MEDICINE; PROFESSOR OF PHYSIOLOGY TO THE PHILADELPHIA MUSEUM; MEMBER OF THE ACADEMY OF NATURAL SCIENCES; HONORARY MEMBER OF THE MEDICAL SOCIETIES OF PHILADEL-PHIA, MARYLAND, BALTIMORE, LEXINGTON, CINCINNATI, PITTSBURG, &c.

Chapter One

FOUNDING A MEDICAL COLLEGE
IN THE CITY OR PRECINCTS OF BALTIMORE

1807~1825

Baltimore 1752

1807

The organizers gathered at Dr. John Davidge's house on the southeast corner of Liberty and Saratoga streets in downtown Baltimore. It was December 28, 1807, just ten days after the Maryland legislature approved a bill establishing their medical college. The act provided legal protection for the enterprise, but no guarantee of success, especially given Davidge's recent ordeal. Teaching an anatomy course in a building erected on his property, the doctor was confronted by angry protestors who demolished the structure and its contents. Davidge was unharmed but received little sympathy for his loss of property. The episode, however, enraged and united the medical community. And the legislation that ensued was the result of their intensive lobbying efforts to establish a medical college with the guarantee of the state.

Conditions for practicing medicine hadn't improved much since 1799 when the state established the Medical and Chirurgical Faculty of Maryland. Its board of medical examiners was charged with regulating the profession, but eight years later fewer than 50 of the 257 members possessed medical degrees. As a result, attempts by the minority to establish a medical college in 1801 and 1802 had failed miserably.

The environment was equally tense beyond Maryland's borders, as only three medical colleges had opened since the founding of the University of Pennsylvania in 1765. Medical doctors were competing for patients with barber-surgeons, street corner apothecaries, and certain clergymen. They also fought popular will, which violently opposed the act of dissecting cadavers— a necessary component of a proper medical education. It didn't help their cause that at times, when available specimens ran short, doctors turned to grave robbers for assistance.

Baltimore was a thriving community in the early 19th century. Endowed with a natural harbor, the city owed much of its prosperity to its accessible location on the Chesapeake Bay. Its 40,000 residents made Baltimore the union's third-largest city. But, like other populated areas, it lacked adequate sanitation. Infectious diseases such as cholera, malaria, tuberculosis, diphtheria, typhus, and typhoid fever were prevalent. And while convenient for travel and transport, the harbor was a breeding ground for mosquitoes—the unrecognized vector of yellow fever. Treating patients for conditions such as infectious diseases, dropsy (edema), or scirrhus (cancer) was largely ineffective. Clinical diagnosis was still in its infancy. There were no thermometers, stethoscopes, antiseptics, or anesthesia. The depletion theory and its methods (cupping, purging, blistering, and bleeding) as well as the available medications (mercury, opium, and arsenic) were at best primitive and at worst harmful. A smallpox epidemic in a community could be devastating. As a result, the average life expectancy was only 34 years, weighted down by a 30 percent infant mortality rate.

However, with the passage of this recent legislation, Maryland legislators had taken a giant step forward in aiding the advancement of organized medicine. There was reason to be

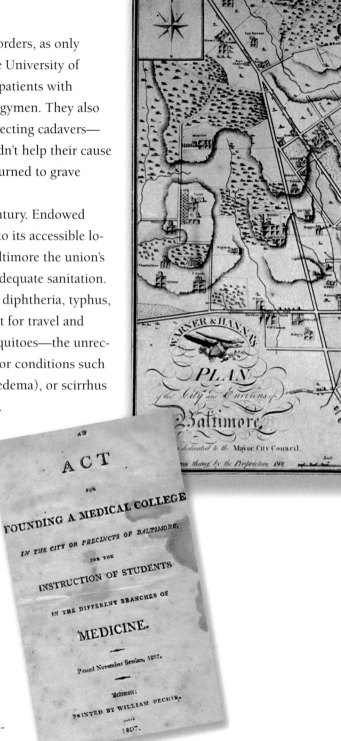

Warner & Hanna's Plan of the City 1801

The act establishing the College of Medicine of Maryland on December 18, 1807, granted unprecedented authority to a board of regents.

hopeful. The act establishing the College of Medicine of Maryland on December 18, 1807, granted unprecedented authority to a board of regents. They answered to no one, being a completely independent group responsible for educating and graduating Maryland physicians. The regents consisted of the state board of medical examiners, the president of the college, and its professors.

The group elected **Dr. George Brown** as president and also appointed him to the professorship of practice and theory of medicine. He immediately resigned his professorship and on his motion, **Dr. Nathaniel Potter** was elected as a replacement. **Drs. John Davidge** and **James Cocke** were appointed to the joint professorship of anatomy, surgery and physiology; **Dr. John Shaw** to the professorship of chemistry; **Dr. Thomas E. Bond** to the professorship of materia medica (pharmacology); and **Dr. William Donaldson** to the professorship of the institutes of medicine (medicine and physiology). Members agreed to resume classes in their homes but for the time being suspended dissections. Clinical instruction was to be taught at the Almshouse on Biddle and Eutaw Streets. Finally, in a fitting tribute to the man who started the medical college in his home, the group elected Davidge as dean of the faculty.

Dr. John Beale Davidge

(Dean 1807-12, 1813-14, 1821-22)

John Beale Davidge was born and raised in Annapolis. His father was an ex-captain in the British army, and his mother was a relative of Col. John Eager Howard. After earning a degree from St. John's College, Davidge studied medicine in Scotland, devoting himself to the study of anatomy and earning a medical degree from the University of Glasgow in 1793. He practiced for a short time in Birmingham, England, before returning to Maryland. After brief stays in Frederick and Harford counties, Davidge arrived in Baltimore in 1796. A yellow fever epidemic raged in the city the following year, and Davidge became a central figure in the public discussion of the disease. In 1801, the Baltimore General Dispensary was founded, and Davidge was named one of its first attending physicians. The following year he offered a private course of lectures to medical students. These annual courses continued until 1807 when his school was formally recognized as The College of Medicine of Maryland.

Davidge had blue eyes and a homely, rosy complexion. He was short and stout with small hands and feet. He had rugged features but a graceful presence. He walked with a slight limp after slipping on the ice and fracturing his leg during the winter of 1818. He was scrupulously neat in his dress, and his manners were immaculate and dignified. As an orator he was slow and cautious, and colleagues described his lectures as "models of simple elegance." Although possessing a certain "irritability of temper," he was beloved by acquaintances and revered by his students who referred to him as "The Father of the University."

He earned a place of prominence in history for many medical advances. In 1823, Davidge performed the world's first extirpation of the parotid gland. He was the first surgeon in the country to tie the gluteal artery for the "cure" of aneurysm, and he was recognized for his ligature of the carotid artery for "fungus of the antrum." Davidge invented a new method of amputation which he referred to as the "American Method."

In 1798, Davidge published *Treatise on Yellow Fever*. An outspoken critic of Benjamin Rush's theory of unity of disease (the belief that all diseases were based in blood vessels and therefore the best treatment was excessive bleeding of patients), Davidge condemned his theories and published his own classification of diseases in *Nosologia Methodica*, released in 1812 with a second edition in 1813. He also published two volumes of *Physical Sketches* in 1814 and 1816; and *Treatise on Amputation* in 1818. He served as editor for *Bancroft on Fevers* in 1821, and a quarterly journal, *Baltimore Philosophical Journal and Review*, in 1823.

Davidge died in 1829 from a malignant tumor of the face. He was survived by his second wife, one son from his first marriage, and three daughters from his second. ཀ

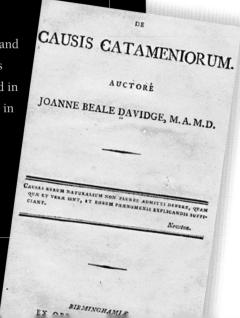

Dr. Thomas E. Bond

1808

⋔ The college's original seven students experienced a rough first session. Dr. Donaldson, professor of the institutes of medicine, and Dr. Bond, professor of materia medica, withdrew from their positions due to ill health. Dr. Shaw's health also failed before the close of the session, and he died in January 1809. With Dr. Potter not expecting to begin his teaching until December 1808, the only lectures completed during the session were those which had begun prior to the College's founding on December 18.

⋔ The faculty was denied state funds to construct a medical building, but received permission to conduct a lottery in an attempt to raise $40,000 in financing. The effort was increased to $100,000 but failed due to the lack of public support, and subsequent efforts were only partially successful.

> " This evening Dr. Crawford of Baltimore drank tea with me . . . The doctor said he had lost all his business by propagating an unpopular opinion in medicine, namely, that all diseases were occasioned by animalculae. He said he was sixty-two years of age and not worth a cent, but in debt."
>
> *Dr. Benjamin Rush*

A LECTURE, INTRODUCTORY TO A COURSE OF LECTURES ON THE CAUSE, SEAT AND CURE OF DISEASES. PROPOSED TO BE DELIVERED IN THE CITY OF BALTIMORE, BY JOHN CRAWFORD, M. D. Baltimore: PUBLISHED BY EDWARD J. COALE. Benjamin Edes, printer. 1811.

⋔ In April the medical school graduated its first class of five students. They were believed to be among those licensed to practice by the faculty. The names included **Francis Cooksey, George T. Gunby, James Orrick, William H. Dorsey**, and either **Robert W. Armstrong** or **Handy Harris Irving**.

1810

1811

⋔ **Dr. John Crawford** began teaching courses on natural history at the medical college. His introductory lecture, "The Cause, Seat, and Cure of Diseases" correctly predicted a relationship between insects and human illness, and he published his concepts in a monograph. A medical graduate of the University of Leyden, Crawford conceived of the germ theory while residing in South America around 1790. He received praise for being among the first in America to administer a viral vaccine (for smallpox) in 1800. This work, in Baltimore, was done simultaneously with Dr. Waterhouse of Massachusetts. Unfortunately colleagues and patients rejected his radical germ theory, leaving Crawford destitute and isolated. He died in 1813.

The medical college was re-chartered by the state as the University of Maryland and was "authorized to constitute, appoint and annex to itself faculties of divinity, law, and arts & sciences." It became the first university in America to be founded with a medical school at its educational core. Financed by members of the faculty, a medical building was erected on land owned by John Eager Howard on the corner of Lombard and Greene streets. The building opened for classes in the lower lecture hall in November. The construction cost totaled just under $40,000, and the underlying land was finally purchased by the regents in 1815 for the sum of $8,887.50.

ᔕ **Dr. Nathaniel Potter** was named dean.

1812

Erected by the Medical Faculty of M.d
Corner of Lombard and Greene Streets. After the Parthenon of Athens Estimated Cost 200,000 D.

From Poppleton's map of Baltimore, Circa 1822

Potter's Memoir on Contagion

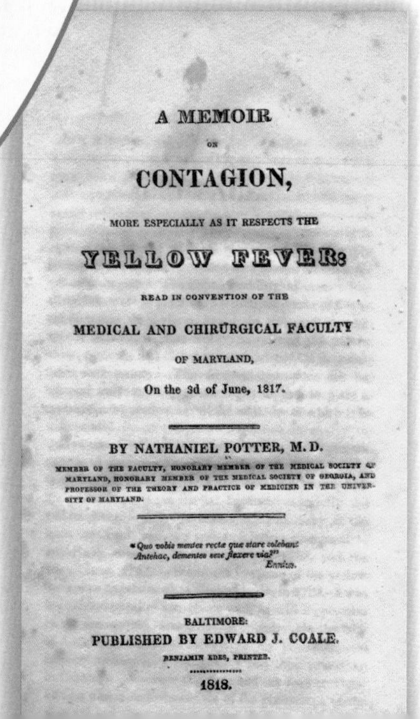

A MEMOIR
ON
CONTAGION,
MORE ESPECIALLY AS IT RESPECTS THE
YELLOW FEVER:
READ IN CONVENTION OF THE
MEDICAL AND CHIRURGICAL FACULTY
OF MARYLAND,
On the 3d of June, 1817.

BY NATHANIEL POTTER, M.D.
MEMBER OF THE FACULTY, HONORARY MEMBER OF THE MEDICAL SOCIETY OF
MARYLAND, HONORARY MEMBER OF THE MEDICAL SOCIETY OF GEORGIA, AND
PROFESSOR OF THE THEORY AND PRACTICE OF MEDICINE IN THE UNIVER-
SITY OF MARYLAND.

*Quo nobis mentes recte que stare solebant
Antehac, dementes sese fixere viâ.*
Ennius.

BALTIMORE:
PUBLISHED BY EDWARD J. COALE.
BENJAMIN EDES, PRINTER.
1818.

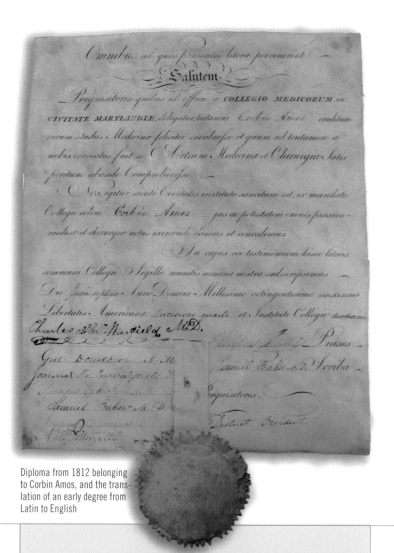

Diploma from 1812 belonging to Corbin Amos, and the translation of an early degree from Latin to English

Dr. Nathaniel Potter

(Dean 1812–13, 1814–15)

Nathaniel Potter, a native of Easton, Maryland, was born in 1770. He was the son of Zabdiel Potter, a surgeon in the Continental Army during the Revolutionary War.

Potter received his medical degree from the University of Pennsylvania in 1796, where his mentor was the noted physician, Dr. Benjamin Rush. Potter was the first American physician to contest the contagion concept of yellow fever. To strengthen his argument, he slept with a towel wrapped around his face containing secretions of his yellow fever patients and did not contract the disease.

Arriving in Baltimore in 1797, Potter became the school's first chair of theory and practice in 1807, a post he held until his death nearly 40 years later. A distinguished lecturer and physician with a large private medical practice, Potter's popular classroom declaration was "I'm damned, gentlemen, if it ain't so."

Potter was president of the Baltimore Medical Society and the Medical Society of Maryland. He also served as both secretary and orator of the Medical and Chirurgical Faculty. A prolific contributor to medical literature, he was recognized for his thesis *An Essay on the Medicinal Properties and Deleterious Qualities of Arsenic*. His 1838 publication, *Some Account of the Rise and Progress of the University of Maryland*, chronicled the early days of the university.

A steadfast supporter of the medical college, Potter contributed more financial support than any of his colleagues to help maintain the institution. At the time of his death in 1843, Potter's financial situation was dismal. His estate had no money for a funeral or grave marker. Contributions from his family and colleagues funded a funeral service, but 150 years would pass before a marker was placed at his grave by members of the Medical Alumni Association. The family homestead, Potter's Landing, still stands near Denton, Maryland. ❧

ACADEMY OF MARYLAND

To all to whose attention this document may come

GREETINGS

Corbineus Amos, a man of many of the finest and the highest talents, has completed his full course of study in the medical arts. He then came before this honorable faculty declaring himself ready for examination in the area of medicine and we have examined him thoroughly and extensively in that area.

In our examination we found him to be highly capable in the sciences and the healing arts and agreed that said Corbineus Amos is worthy to be made and declared a Doctor of Medicine. Through this document we declare and establish that he is a Doctor and is to be considered and called such by all.

We bestow upon him the fullest entitlement to teach and to consult in medical matters and to fill positions in both theoretical and practical medicine anywhere upon the earth.

He is entitled to all the honors, rights, and privileges which our society bestows on a Doctor of Medicine.

To validate this document which bears the seal of the Academy, we have added our signatures. Given in the city of Baltimore on the 15th day of April in the year of our Lord, 1812.

Charles A. Warfield, President
John B. Davidge, MD
James Cocke, MD
Elisha DeButts, MD
Nathaniel Potter, MD
Samuel Baker, MD

1815

🔊 A medical library opened on the first floor of the medical building. It was created after a purchase of the collection owned by the late Dr. John Crawford. The 500 volumes were acquired from Crawford's family.

1814

🔊 **Samuel Martin**, class of 1813, made a daring rescue during the War of 1812. As American troops were repelling the British during the Battle of North Point in Baltimore, Sgt. Alexander MacKenzie lay wounded on the battlefield. Martin, riding horseback, charged in, scooped up MacKenzie and carried him to safety. It was during this critical battle that Major General Robert Ross, commander of the British forces, was mortally wounded.

1816

🔊 **Dr. Elisha DeButts** was named dean.

Dr. Elisha DeButts
(Dean 1816–17, 1822–25)

Born in Dublin, Ireland, in 1773, Elisha DeButts immigrated with his family to America when he was a young boy. He began studying medicine with his uncle, Dr. Samuel DeButts, and later enrolled at the University of Pennsylvania for his formal medical training.

Considered one of the most brilliant chemists of his day, DeButts was credited with much of the medical school's rapid growth during his tenure as chair of chemistry, a position he held for more than 20 years beginning in 1809. Students and fellow faculty maintained that DeButts' abilities were unsurpassed by his contemporaries.

An accomplished musician, artist and poet, DeButts was also an eloquent speaker. His ability to make even the driest subject matter interesting to an audience attracted large crowds wherever he spoke. On a mission to purchase chemical equipment for the school, DeButts traveled to Europe, where he lectured before the Royal Institution of London. He died of pneumonia in 1831. 🔊

Dr. William Gibson

(Dean 1818–19)

William Gibson was born in Baltimore in 1788. He was educated at St. John's College and Princeton University and spent a short time at the medical school of the University of Pennsylvania. Gibson earned a medical degree from the University of Edinburgh in 1809, and studied with Sir Charles Bell in London before returning to Baltimore. While traveling in Europe, he was an observer at the Battle of Waterloo and was slightly wounded during the fighting. He also played a visible role in the War of 1812, extracting a musket ball from the body of General Scott during the Battle of Lundy's Lane, near Niagara Falls.

A bold operator, Gibson became the first surgeon in the world to successfully ligate the common iliac artery in 1812. The operation was performed on a man shot in the lower abdomen during a political riot protesting America's war declaration. This was the first demonstration of the establishment of collateral circulation of the lower extremity after the ligation of a major artery. Later, Gibson was first in the U.S. to divide the recti muscles of the eye for correction of strabismus. Presumably, he failed to pursue this procedure further; thus he was not generally acknowledged as the pioneer in America for this surgical technique. Gibson performed the world's first successful repeat Caesarian operation, a truly notable achievement given the circumstances—before the utilization of antisepsis and surgical anesthesia.

In 1812 at the age of 23, Gibson was elected chair of surgery at Maryland. His presence was a great attraction for the young school. Seven years later he accepted the chair of surgery at the University of Pennsylvania where he remained until 1855. In his later years, Gibson received an honorary LLD degree from the University of Edinburgh. His most noted publication, *The Institutes and Practice of Surgery*, advanced through nine editions. His journals, filling 150 volumes, were lost after his death.

Gibson was a well-rounded individual: an accomplished surgeon, scholar, sportsman, artist, musician, writer and traveler. He was also an avid fisherman, botanist, and a distinguished ornithologist. Even in the final year of his life, at the age of 80, Gibson continued to work in his taxidermy shop. ✍

Gibson performed the world's first successful repeat Caesarian operation, a truly notable achievement given the circumstances—before the utilization of antisepsis and surgical anesthesia.

1819

✍ **William Zollicoffer**, class of 1818, was credited with publishing a treatise on materia medica, the first of its kind in America. He later became lecturer in botany, materia medica and toxicology at Maryland.

✍ **Dr. Richard W. Hall** was named dean.

1818

✍ **Dr. William Gibson** was named dean.

Dr. Richard Wilmot Hall

(Dean 1819–20, 1837–39)

The son of Revolutionary War surgeon Jacob Hall, Richard Wilmot Hall was born in Harford County, Maryland, in 1785. He received a medical degree from the University of Pennsylvania in 1806 and settled in Baltimore in 1811. The following year he received an appointment as adjunct professor of obstetrics at the medical school.

Twice the dean at Maryland, Hall played an active role in the affairs of the university during its 13-year struggle with the state and developed many political enemies. Despite his popularity among students, he was impeached in 1843 at a trial held by the Medical and Chirurgical Faculty. Hall vigorously defended himself against faculty detractors who charged him with incompetency and violating regulations. He was subsequently acquitted by the regents and retained his faculty position until his death in 1847 at the age of 62.

In addition to a number of short articles mentioned in John Quinan's *Medical Annals of Baltimore*, Hall authored a two-volume translation of Baron Larrey's *Memoirs of Military Surgery.* ∞

Maxwell McDowell

(Dean 1820–21, 1825–28)

McDowell, a Pennsylvania native, was born in 1771. He was educated at Dickinson College in Carlisle, Pennsylvania, earning an AM degree in 1792. He practiced in York, Pennsylvania, before settling in Baltimore as attending physician to the Baltimore General Dispensary. McDowell was professor of the institutes of medicine at the medical school from 1814 to 1833, and in 1818 received an honorary medical degree from Maryland.

From the earliest years of the medical college, it was customary to take only four classes – anatomy, surgery, chemistry and practice – during the first year of study. As dean, McDowell required that these classes be taken both years by students enrolled in the two-year doctoral course. This requirement remained in force until the graded course was adopted. McDowell authored *Treatment of Burns by Cold Water* and *On the Pathology of Diabetes Mellitus*. He died in 1847 at age 76. ∞

1820

∞ A pioneer surgeon, **Horatio G. Jameson**, class of 1813, successfully excised the entire upper jaw of a cancer patient, the first surgery of its kind in the world. In 1821, he performed Baltimore's first tracheotomy. Two years later, in 1823, he reported the successful removal of a uterine cervix, presumably the first operation of its kind in America and Great Britain. Jameson served as a consulting surgeon to the hospitals of Baltimore City from 1819 to 1835, and as consulting physician to the city's board of health from 1822 to 1835. In 1827, after being denied a faculty appointment at Maryland, he became founder and president of the Washington Medical College in Baltimore. He also served as its professor of surgery and surgical anatomy until 1835. He later became the first president and professor of surgery at Ohio Medical College in Cincinnati. Jameson is also remembered for defending America during the War of 1812, serving as a surgeon to U.S. troops in Baltimore.

∞ **Maxwell McDowell** was named dean.

Jameson's cancer patient

Granville Sharp Pattison

(Dean 1821–22)

Granville Sharp Pattison was born near Glasgow, Scotland, in 1791, and educated at the private anatomical school of Dr. Allan Burns. Although he had no medical degree, Pattison won appointment as professor of anatomy, physiology, and surgery at the Andersonian Institution in Glasgow in 1812.

In 1818, Pattison came to America, opening an anatomical school in Philadelphia after an abbreviated and controversial appointment at the University of Pennsylvania. When he failed to win appointment as chair in anatomy there, Pattison became embroiled in a public argument with his chief detractor, Dr. Nathaniel Chapman. In 1820, Pattison left Philadelphia to become chair of surgery at Maryland and dean the following year, but his ongoing dispute with Chapman culminated two years later in a duel with Chapman's brother-in-law, General Thomas Cadwalader. Pattison escaped without injury—after inflicting a wound that permanently disabled his opponent's right arm. Chapman, in 1847, became the first president of the American Medical Association.

Pattison's impact at Maryland was immediate. Considered one of the most able surgical anatomy teachers of his time, he was an inspiring influence on both students and colleagues. His personal energy and charisma infused new life into a university that, upon his arrival, was burdened with debt and an unfinished medical building already in need of repair. During Pattison's tenure at Maryland, enrollment experienced its most significant gains, and the school became a successful rival of the University of Pennsylvania. The school's resources were enhanced significantly when it purchased from Pattison a large anatomical collection shipped from Scotland. Shortly afterwards, the legislature advanced a $30,000 loan to repair and complete the medical building and to build Practice Hall, a small addition to house the anatomical museum. Under his guidance, the Infirmary was constructed one year after his deanship.

In 1820, Pattison published the first description of the fascia of the prostate gland. This account resulted in the improvement of vesicoperineal lithotomy. He was editor of *The Register and Library of Medical and Chirurgical Science*, two editions of Burns' *Observations on the Surgical Anatomy of the Arteries of the Head and Neck*, Masse's atlas of anatomical plates, and Cruveilhier's *Anatomy*.

After leaving Maryland in 1826, Pattison traveled abroad to fill the chair of anatomy at the London University. He returned to America in 1832, winning appointment as professor of anatomy at Jefferson Medical College. He later joined in founding the medical department of New York University and received an honorary medical degree late in life. He died in 1851. ∽

Pattison was perhaps the most colorful faculty member in the history of the medical school.

1821

∽ **Granville S. Pattison** was named dean.

A specimen from Pattison's anatomical collection

A page from a student's hospital log

1823

Maryland became the first medical school in the U.S. to build its own hospital for clinical instruction. During this time most schools were placing more emphasis on classroom instruction, neglecting clinical education, but Drs. Cocke and Davidge believed it very important to give students regular tours through local hospitals. Dr. Pattison lobbied for an infirmary to provide proper clinical training. After refusals from the banks and city for financing, he persuaded the faculty to extend their personal credit for the cause. The 60-bed Baltimore Infirmary was constructed at a cost of $14,109 and required $2,520 for furnishings. Pattison recruited nurses from the Sisters of Charity order from Mount St. Mary's in Emmitsburg, Maryland. The dedicated nuns staffed the infirmary for more than 40 years.

Dr. George Frick

🔖 **Dr. George Frick**, lecturer in clinical medicine at Maryland, published the first treatise on eye disease in America. Born in Baltimore in 1793, Dr. Frick was the first in America to restrict his professional work to ophthalmology. He earned his medical degree from the University of Pennsylvania in 1815 and was uncle to Dr. Charles Frick, later a distinguished teacher of materia medica at Maryland.

🔖 In an elaborate ceremony in Anatomical Hall, the **Marquis de Lafayette** received the first non-medical honorary degree bestowed by the University of Maryland—a doctor of laws—on October 9.

1824

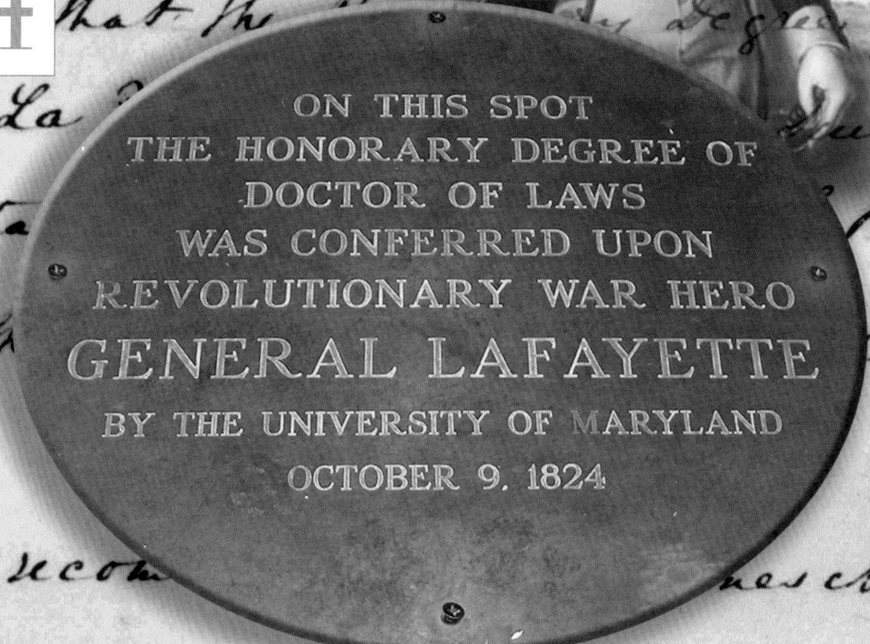

ON THIS SPOT
THE HONORARY DEGREE OF
DOCTOR OF LAWS
WAS CONFERRED UPON
REVOLUTIONARY WAR HERO
GENERAL LAFAYETTE
BY THE UNIVERSITY OF MARYLAND
OCTOBER 9, 1824

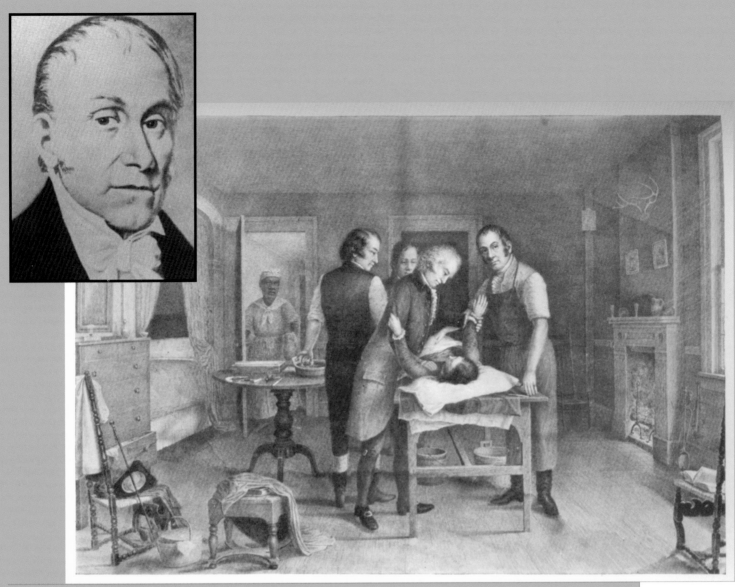

A rendering of the historic procedure. From left are Dr. Cotter, one of McDowell's associates; W. McDowell, a nephew of Ephraim; Dr. Alban Gold Smith, who assisted McDowell; and Ephraim McDowell.

1825

Ephraim McDowell, acclaimed by many as "The Father of Abdominal Surgery," received an honorary medical degree from Maryland, the only degree he ever received. On Christmas Day, 1809, in Danville, Kentucky, he removed a 20-pound abdominal tumor together with its gelatinous fluid from the abdomen of Jane Crawford, who not only survived the procedure but enjoyed good health for 30 more years. While other medical schools and associations were debating the wisdom of McDowell's courageous adventure in surgery, Maryland's faculty had the vision to understand its significance and conferred its honor upon him.

∞ **John D. Godman**, class of 1818, published *Contributions to Physiological and Pathological Anatomy*, the first monograph on pathological anatomy published in the U.S. An orphan who was apprenticed to a printer, Godman ran away and joined the American fleet in the Chesapeake Bay during the War of 1812. After the war, he enrolled at Maryland where his medical talents were immediately recognized. In 1817, while still a student, he was called upon by the faculty to teach a course in anatomy after his instructor, Dr. Davidge, was immobilized by a broken leg. After graduation, Godman opened a school of anatomy in Philadelphia where he held several professorships and lectureships. He served as editor for a number of medical journals, among them the *American Journal of the Medical Sciences*, the most important periodical of its time, and he authored three editions of *Natural History*, the first written work on this subject in America. Godman died of tuberculosis in 1830 at age 35.

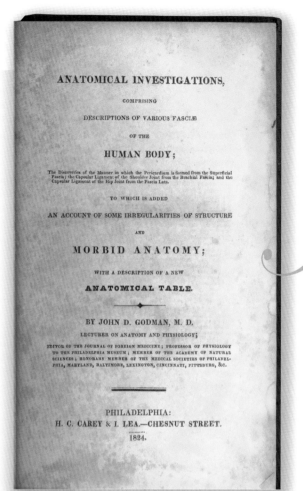

ANATOMICAL INVESTIGATIONS,

COMPRISING

DESCRIPTIONS OF VARIOUS FASCIÆ

OF THE

HUMAN BODY;

The Discoveries of the Manner in which the Pericardium is formed from the Superficial Fascia; the Capsular Ligament of the Shoulder Joint from the Brachial Fascia; and the Capsular Ligament of the Hip Joint from the Fascia Lata.

TO WHICH IS ADDED

AN ACCOUNT OF SOME IRREGULARITIES OF STRUCTURE

AND

MORBID ANATOMY;

WITH A DESCRIPTION OF A NEW

ANATOMICAL TABLE.

BY JOHN D. GODMAN, M. D.

LECTURER ON ANATOMY AND PHYSIOLOGY;

EDITOR OF THE JOURNAL OF FOREIGN MEDICINE; PROFESSOR OF PHYSIOLOGY TO THE PHILADELPHIA MUSEUM; MEMBER OF THE ACADEMY OF NATURAL SCIENCES; HONORARY MEMBER OF THE MEDICAL SOCIETIES OF PHILADELPHIA, MARYLAND, BALTIMORE, LEXINGTON, CINCINNATI, PITTSBURG, &c.

PHILADELPHIA:

H. C. CAREY & I. LEA.—CHESNUT STREET.

1824.

In just 18 years, enrollment at the medical college had increased from seven to 300. One third were Baltimore residents; another third came from rural Maryland, particularly the Eastern Shore and southern Maryland; and the final third traveled to Baltimore from outside the state—areas including Washington, D.C., Virginia, and Pennsylvania, plus small percentages from other states and abroad.

The average age of a Maryland medical student was 20. There were no admissions requirements, and only about 10 percent of applicants had attended college. It was often the case that a student had served an extensive apprenticeship prior to enrolling. All were male and could afford the relatively expensive fees for classes.

To enroll, a student paid a $5 matriculation fee to the university plus $20 each to the professors for enrolling in their courses; a signed lecture ticket ensured admission for the session. Two degrees were offered: a one-year bachelor of medicine (offered through 1848); and a two-year doctor of medicine. While getting in was easy, getting out was more difficult, as candidates for graduation were required to write a thesis and pass both public and private examinations.

In the eyes of the community, the University of Maryland seemed to be thriving. But trouble was brewing, and many people, including insiders, were soon surprised by actions announced by the state legislature.

Dr. John D. Godman

Chapter Two

1826-1859

otter was visibly shaken. A founding regent, he was in Annapolis on a March day
to lobby for university interests: namely, to advocate against a proposal establishing
a competing medical school in Baltimore, the Washington Medical College. Upon
entering the State House, he heard chatter that the legislature was about to take over the University of Maryland. Potter immediately became suspicious of his traveling companion, Dr. Elisha
DeButts, who remained surprisingly composed upon hearing the news.

DeButts had joined the faculty in 1809, succeeding Shaw. The chemistry professor was held in high
esteem by both faculty and students, but he had been dissatisfied with the university's progress recently
and had complained about it to at least one colleague. The medical building, he argued, had never been
satisfactorily completed; the university and its faculty
were in debt, and the morale of their colleagues was
at its lowest ebb since the school's founding.

The state did come
through with a $30,000
loan in 1821 to refurbish
and complete the medical
building, but it had to be
backed by the personal
bond of faculty members.
In addition to the financial pressures, the faculty
was bitterly divided over
activities of DeButts and
Davidge. Even though
classes had moved into
the newly constructed
medical building in 1812,
the two continued to offer
popular evening classes
out of their homes—
classes that often
included material taught
at the medical school by
fellow faculty: a recipe for
disaster. Opponents
wanted the unapproved
classes halted. They

An artist's illustration of the struggle for control of the University of Maryland

EDICAL CONVERSATIONS,

EVERY

EDNESDAY & SATURDAY NIGHT,

At eight of the clock,

BY

OHN B. DAVIDGE, M. D.

called a vote on the matter at a faculty meeting and the outcome was decisive. Davidge and DeButts lost, 12–6.

Criticism also mounted that the medical department was squandering all of the university's funds. This would be a direct violation of the university charter approved in 1812, which called for the institution to annex to itself faculties of divinity, law, and arts & sciences. Potter understood the power of this accusation, and had little to say in defense. Despite the appointment of five leading Protestant clergymen to the faculty of divinity in 1812, the department had never materialized. Only one set of theology lectures had been offered during the session of 1823. In addition, the law department had but one faculty member and absolutely nothing had been done to establish a department of arts & sciences.

In a conversation with regent David Hoffman, Maryland's sole law professor, DeButts concluded that the institution could not last more than one session unless rescued by the legislature. With allegations of mismanagement and the likelihood of a competing medical school in town, Potter began preparing for the fight of his life.

On March 26, through the passage of a bill, the legislature stripped the regents of their authority, transferring power to the governor who would serve as president, and a 21-member state-appointed board of trustees. All faculty members with the exception of the professors were dismissed, and the trustees were given authority to appoint or dismiss faculty at their pleasure. Professors could nominate candidates to fill vacancies, but the trustees were not bound to accept them. Adding insult to injury, the professors and many of the faculty were informed that they were not entitled to recover their personal funds invested in the institution, yet they were not released from payment of interest on the $30,000 state loan made in 1821.

Potter and the regents fought back. Their legal counsel included William Wirt, a well known U.S. attorney general; John Purviance, a prominent Baltimore attorney; and Daniel Webster, a rising star in the U.S. House of Representatives. The team declared the act of 1826 to

In a conversation with regent David Hoffman, Maryland's sole law professor, DeButts concluded that the institution could not last more than one session unless rescued by the legislature. With allegations of mismanagement and the likelihood of a competing medical school in town, Potter began preparing for the fight of his life.

CIRCULAR

OF THE

REGENTS' MEDICAL FACULTY

OF THE

UNIVERSITY OF MARYLAND.

THE Faculty of Physic in the University of Maryland (under the Board of Regents) on the present occasion address themselves to the early friends and alumni of this institution, with peculiar claims to their patronage and support.

The public need scarcely be told that the Medical School of the University of Maryland owes its origin to the private enterprise and industry of its professors. By their toil, their talent, and the liberal appropriation of their pecuniary means it was fostered and maintained, until it became an honour to its projectors, the pride of the State, and abundantly useful to the public. More than three hundred pupils annually frequented its halls, and it vied with the most flourishing institutions of our country. Thus far the Medical Faculty governed the school, and although differences of opinion necessarily arose yet nothing occurred to mar its prosperity.

At length a disaffected minority of the Faculty displeased with an act of that body, in an evil hour applied to the legislature of Maryland to modify the government of the school. Although the charter previously granted was perpetual and immutable, yet the legislature not properly considering the unconstitutionality of the act, granted the petition, and wresting the government from the hands of those who had brought the school into existence, placed it wholly in the hands of a Board of Trustees, not even leaving to the professors the power of controlling their own pupils. They were no longer allowed

Webster's legal opinion from the faculty minutes

I concur, entirely, in opinion with the attorney General & Mr Purviance. The Regents of the University were authorized by the grant of the Legislature, to exercise certain privileges & to acquire & hold property. An act, intended to abolish those privileges, without forfeiture, & to transfer that property to others, strikes me as being plainly repugnant to the grant itself, and therefore void by the constitution of the United States.

Daniel Webster.

be a "manifest violation" of the acts of 1807 and 1812, arguing that it violated an article of the U.S. Constitution forbidding any state from passing a law which impairs the obligation of a contract.

The initial ruling of the court went against the regents; so the trustees took possession of the grounds, giving the professors 15 days to apply for reappointment to their positions. Virtually all of them did. It would be a stormy relationship between the trustees and many of the defunct regents for the next several years. If Davidge and DeButts did encourage the takeover, they certainly didn't benefit from it, as their appeal to teach additional classes from their homes was denied. Davidge died in 1829, surrounded by professional conflict.

The crisis continued for several years and reached its peak on May 2, 1837, when a number of faculty resigned. These were the individuals who had worked under the old system. Potter and Hall announced that their resignations were limited to the trustees' school and they were retaining their former appointments under the original charter. They reappointed faculty to their former positions and reopened the old school at the Indian Queen Hotel, located at Baltimore and Hanover streets.

There were now two schools operating as the University of Maryland. The combined enrollments were disappointing, as the student body was split over which school to attend. Most Baltimore residents transferred to the old regent-guided school, while their out-of-town colleagues stayed with the trustees. Others departed for the Washington Medical College which had opened downtown in 1827. Several faculty members from the two University of Maryland campuses also expressed their displeasure by resigning.

Finally, in 1839, after 13 years of hostilities and two years of competing schools, the Maryland Court of Appeals settled the matter by reversing the lower court decision. The act of 1826 was declared unconstitutional in violation of the U.S. Constitution, Bill of Rights, and the constitution of the State of Maryland. The court ruled that the university had none of the characteristics of a public corporation, and the university property and funds did not belong to the state. The rights under the original charters of 1807 and 1812 could not be acquired, the court concluded, without the permission of the regents. Authority was transferred back to the regents on April 10.

Potter later concluded that Davidge and DeButts had made a terrible mistake in judgment.

The Washington Medical College

ᔕ The Washington Medical College opened in Baltimore, granted authority by Washington College in Washington, Pennsylvania, and approval of the state of Maryland. Located on Holliday Street opposite City Hall, this was Maryland's first rival medical school in the city, later known as the Washington University School of Medicine. It merged with the Baltimore College of Physicians and Surgeons in 1877.

1828

ᔕ **Dr. Nathan R. Smith** was named dean.

Dr. Nathan Ryno Smith

(Dean 1828–30, 1841–42)

Born in Cornish, New Hampshire, in 1797, Nathan Ryno Smith was tutored in Virginia and earned his medical degree from Yale in 1823. He was the son of Dr. Nathan Smith, a distinguished surgeon and a founder of both Dartmouth and Yale medical schools. The younger Smith established the medical department at the University of Vermont, where he served as professor of surgery and anatomy. He later accepted an appointment for two sessions as professor of anatomy at Jefferson Medical College, which he helped organize.

A leading surgeon of his era, Smith accepted the chair of surgery at Maryland in 1827, commencing an eventful 50-year career in Baltimore. Considered a bold and skillful surgeon, Smith was known to his students as "The Emperor." He was the first to resect the parotid gland for a neoplasm, and he performed the second operation in the U.S. for removal of a goiter.

Smith was widely recognized as the inventor of the anterior splint for fractures of the lower extremities. The device was perfected in 1860 and adapted for general use in America and abroad. A valuable tool for the treatment of compound fractures, the splint saw extensive use during the Civil War. Smith himself regarded the invention as his most important contribution to medicine.

Recognized throughout the world for his medical acumen, Smith was lauded in Gross' *A Century of American Medicine.* In a chapter on surgery, Gross referred to Smith as "one of the greatest surgeons America has produced." Smith's most significant publications included *Memoirs, Medical and Surgical, of Dr. Nathan Smith, with Additions by the Author* in 1837; *Surgical Anatomy of the Arteries* in 1830; and *Fractures of the Lower Extremity and Use of Suspensory Apparatus* in 1867. He died in 1877 at the age of 80. ᔕ

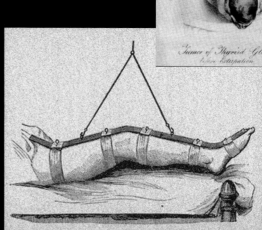

Smith's goiter patient (above) and splint (below)

1828

A duel was fought between students Samuel Carr of South Carolina and William Martin of the Eastern Shore over the affections of Mary Polk, stepdaughter of John Davidge. The men settled their dispute at the Bladensburg dueling grounds when Carr, an experienced duelist, killed Martin with a bullet between the eyes. He was expelled from medical school. He eloped with Miss Polk, and the couple left the state. Carr returned several years later and resumed his medical studies, graduating in 1834.

1829

Dr. Samuel Baker was named dean.

Dr. Samuel Baker

(Dean 1829–31)

Born in Baltimore in 1785, Samuel Baker studied at Chestertown Academy on the Eastern Shore. He graduated with a degree in medicine from the University of Pennsylvania in 1808. The following year, he was elected to the chair of materia medica at Maryland.

Baker served as president of the Baltimore Medical Society and its successor, the Medical Society of Baltimore, and as president and secretary of the Medical and Chirurgical Faculty. During his tenure as chairman of the board of directors of the library of the Medical and Chirurgical Faculty, Baker started the library's valuable collection with a $500 contribution. He continued to preside over the board and to take great interest in the library throughout his lifetime.

Baker was an amiable and excellent physician who devoted his professional life to advancing the medical school. Two of his sons, William N. Baker and Samuel George Baker, also served as professors at Maryland. The elder Baker died of heart disease in 1835, only six years before the untimely deaths of both sons.

Dr. Eli Geddings

(Dean 1832–34, 1836–37)

Born in South Carolina in 1799, Eli Geddings began the study of medicine in 1818, and attended his first formal lectures at the University of Pennsylvania two years later. Geddings was one of the first graduates of the Medical College of South Carolina, receiving his medical degree in 1825. Following further study in London and Paris, he arrived in Baltimore.

Geddings was considered an intelligent man and a capable teacher as well as a formidable writer. Praised by his colleagues for his brilliance and skill, Geddings' election as chair of anatomy and physiology at Maryland was unanimous. Fluent in 14 languages, he served as editor of the *Baltimore Medical Journal* and founded the *Baltimore Medical and Surgical Journal and Review*, a quarterly publication which later became the *North American Archives of Medical and Surgical Science*. Geddings was also a valuable contributor to the *American Journal of the Medical Sciences*.

Despite offers of professorships from several medical colleges, Geddings returned to the Medical College of South Carolina in Charleston, where a chair of pathological anatomy and medical jurisprudence was created for him. When medical courses were suspended during the Civil War, Geddings accepted an appointment as a surgeon in the Confederate Army. His entire library, considered one of the finest private collections in the country, was sent to Columbia for safe-keeping, but did not survive General William T. Sherman's torching of the city. Following the war, Geddings was instrumental in reviving the Medical College of South Carolina, where he assumed the chair of surgery. He died in 1878.

The medical building with Practice Hall on the right

1833

Maryland established a medical course in preventive medicine, the first in America. The course was conceived and taught by Dr. Robley Dunglison, professor of materia medica and therapeutics, hygiene and medical jurisprudence from 1833 to 1836.

The schedule of student Thomas McGill: Arrive at the Infirmary at 9 am; follow Dr. Potter through rounds to inspect medical cases on Mondays and Wednesdays; Tuesdays and Thursdays follow Dr. Smith to inspect surgical cases; attend surgery lectures at 10 am Monday through Friday; materia medica lectures at 11 am; theory and practice lectures at noon; anatomy lectures at 1 pm; dinner break from 2–4 pm; obstetrics at 4 pm; chemistry at 5 pm; and after 6 pm spent an hour or more in the dissecting lab.

1832

Dr. Eli Geddings was named dean.

1834

Dr. Robley Dunglison was named dean.

25

Dr. Robley Dunglison

(Dean 1834–36)

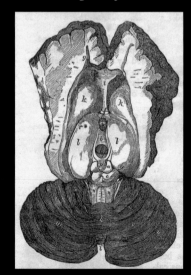

Robley Dunglison was born in England in 1798. He studied medicine at the universities of Edinburgh and Paris, and was a licentiate of the Royal College of Surgeons and Apothecaries in London. In 1824, Dunglison received his medical degree from the University of Erlangen in Germany and, one year later, an honorary medical degree from Yale. In 1825, at the invitation of Thomas Jefferson, he founded the University of Virginia School of Medicine, where he was faculty chair and professor of anatomy, physiology, materia medica, and pharmacy. Later, Dunglison was made professor of the institutes of medicine and dean of the faculty at Jefferson Medical College in Philadelphia. He received the degree of LLD from both Yale and Jefferson College in Canonsburg, Pennsylvania.

At Maryland, Dunglison was dean of the faculty from 1834 to 1835. He also served as the physician to four U.S. presidents: Jefferson, Madison, Monroe and Jackson.

One of the country's most prolific medical writers, Dunglison published numerous volumes and regularly contributed to periodical literature. His *Elements of Hygiene,* published in 1833, was the first work of its kind on preventive medicine in the world. And his best-known work, *Medical Dictionary,* enjoyed more than 20 editions. He also published *Human Physiology and Practice of Medicine.* By 1858, sales of his principal books were reputed to exceed 100,000 volumes.

Described by Dr. Samuel D. Gross as "a beacon of light in the world of medical literature," Dunglison died in 1869. The medical school commemorates his contributions each year at commencement by conferring upon a graduating student the Robley Dunglison Award for Excellence in Preventive Medicine. ಐ

Dunglison's description of the cerebrum from his 1850 edition of *Human Physiology*

Dunglison served as the physician to four U.S. presidents: Jefferson, Madison, Monroe and Jackson.

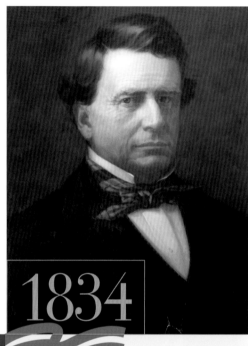

1834

ಐ **John Wesley Davis**, class of 1821, was elected to the U.S. Congress from Carlisle, Indiana. He served three additional terms and, during the 29th Congress, Davis was appointed Speaker of the House. President Polk appointed Davis as commissioner to China from 1848 to 1851. He returned to Baltimore in 1852 to serve as president of the Democratic convention that nominated Franklin Pierce. After winning, President Pierce appointed Davis governor of the Oregon Territory. Two years later, Davis retired from public office and returned to Carlisle. He died, nearly destitute, in 1859.

1837

₭ America's first dental lectures were delivered at Maryland by **Dr. Horace H. Hayden**. In 1839, after his request to establish a dental department was denied, Hayden founded the Baltimore College of Dental Surgery, the first of its kind in the world. Years later, in 1882, the college's dean and professor of clinical surgery were invited to serve in these same capacities at Maryland, effecting a hostile takeover of the dental college. The institution formally merged with Maryland in the early 20th century.

1838

₭ **Augustus Lockman Warner**, class of 1829 and Maryland faculty member, founded the Medical College of Virginia in Richmond. He organized the school under the charter of Hampden-Sydney College and served as dean and professor of surgery. Prior to moving to Richmond in 1837, he won appointment as professor of anatomy, physiology and surgery at the University of Virginia in Charlottesville.

₭ **Theodatus Garlick**, class of 1834, snapped the first American photograph, a daguerreotype. Practicing medicine in Youngstown, Ohio, until 1852, Garlick was the first to make anatomical models in plaster for use in medical schools. In 1857, he published a book describing a workable method of artificial propagation of fish (pisciculture). The work became the standard text for increasing the supply of aquatic food, and Garlick was recognized as "The Father of American Fish Culture."

1839

₭ **Samuel G. Baker**, class of 1835, was named dean.

Dr. Samuel George Baker
(Dean 1839–40)

Samuel George Baker, born in Baltimore in 1814, became the first medical school graduate of Maryland to serve as its dean. He was a son of Samuel Baker, dean of Maryland's faculty from 1829 to 1830. The younger Baker received his BA degree from Yale in 1832, earning his medical degree in 1835. Like his father, Samuel G. Baker was elected to the chair of materia medica. At 22, he became the youngest professor the university had ever had. Baker was chosen as dean at the conclusion of the 13-year court battle between the regents and the legislature over control of the university.

Baker and his brother, William (also a faculty member), were handsome, talented and popular young men, but so-called "habits of dissipation" shortened both of their promising careers. Just a few months separated their untimely deaths in 1841—Samuel at age 27 and William at age 30. At the time of his death, Samuel was editor of the *Maryland Medical and Surgical Journal.* ₭

William E. A. Aikin

(Dean 1840–41, 1844–55)

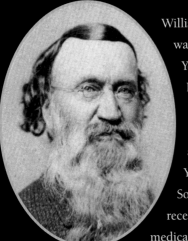

William E. A. Aikin was born in New York in 1807. Educated at Renssalaer Institute and a licentiate of the New York State Medical Society, Aikin received an honorary medical degree from the Vermont Academy of Medicine and an honorary LLD degree from Georgetown University.

Aikin's career as a practitioner of medicine was brief, as he preferred science to the "drudgery" of country practice. Shortly after moving to Maryland in 1832, Aikin joined the chemistry faculty at the medical school. To equip the chemistry laboratory for the regents' school, Aikin was authorized to purchase chemical apparatus on the credit of the faculty.

Aikin's knowledge of his profession was extensive and exact. With a six-foot frame and a flowing white beard, he had a commanding presence. He was married twice and fathered 28 children.

In addition to his post as professor of chemistry, Aikin was professor of natural philosophy in the university's temporary department of arts & sciences, a lecturer at the Maryland Institute, and city inspector of gas and illuminating oils. He contributed articles on chemical, geological, botanical and mineralogical subjects to numerous journals, and developed a valuable list of plants native to Baltimore. He died in 1888. ∞

THE

MARYLAND

MEDICAL AND SURGICAL JOURNAL,

AND

OFFICIAL ORGAN OF THE MEDICAL DEPARTMENT

OF THE

Army and Navy of the United States.

VOLUME I.

Qui ante nos ista moverunt, non domini nostri sed duces sunt. Patet omnibus veritas; nondum est occupata; multum ex illa etiam futuris relictum est.—*Seneca, Epist. 33.*

PUBLISHED UNDER THE AUSPICES OF THE
Medical and Chirurgical Faculty of Maryland.

EDITORIAL COMMITTEE,

G. C. M. ROBERTS, M.D.   ROBERT A. DURKEE, M.D.
NATHANIEL POTTER, M.D.   JOHN R. W. DUNBAR, M.D.
JAMES H. MILLER, M.D.   SAMUEL GEORGE BAKER, M.D.

BALTIMORE:
PRINTED AND PUBLISHED BY JOHN MURPHY,
146 MARKET STREET.
MDCCCXL.

1840

∞ **Dr. William E.A. Aikin** was named dean.

∞ *The Maryland Medical and Surgical Journal,* edited by Maryland's faculty, became the first official publication to be adopted by the medical departments of the U.S. Army and Navy.

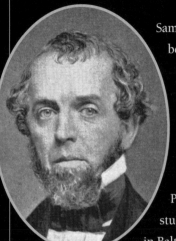

Dr. Samuel Chew
(Dean 1842–44)

Samuel Chew was born in 1806 in Calvert County, Maryland. Educated at Charlotte Hall in St. Mary's City, and at Princeton, Chew studied medicine in Baltimore under Dr. William Donaldson, a prominent physician and one of Maryland's founders. He entered the medical school in 1826 and received his medical degree in 1829.

In 1840, Chew co-founded an eye and ear institute in Baltimore. He was elected professor of therapeutics, materia medica and hygiene at the medical school the following year, and later became chair of principles and practice of medicine, a post he held until his death. Chew also served as librarian, vice president and treasurer of the Medical and Chirurgical Faculty.

Samuel Chew was a man of integrity, recognized for both his charity and his scholarly achievements. His most extensive work, *Lectures on Medical Education*, was written for students. It was unfinished at his death but later completed by his son. Chew practiced medicine for 38 years and died of pneumonia on Christmas Day, 1863, at age 57. ✍

1841

ᔥ **William Power**, class of 1835, introduced Laennec's innovations of auscultation and percussion to Baltimore. His appointments at Maryland followed additional medical studies in Paris under Pierre Louis. Upon his return to America in 1840, Power became resident physician at the Almshouse and after nine months was named its visiting physician. Beginning in 1841, he was invited by Maryland's faculty to deliver two courses of lectures at the infirmary on physical examination of the chest. The talks proved very popular, and Power was named professor of theory and practice of medicine in 1845. He was an exceptional teacher, especially in the clinical setting. Until his appointment at Maryland, it was difficult to secure resident students at the infirmary. Afterwards, applicants waited as long as one year for an opening. It was during his tenure, in 1846, when graduate James Morison became the first resident physician for the infirmary. Power's presence helped restore Maryland's reputation as an excellent medical school, following its battle with the state that left it fragmented and destitute. Power held his appointment until 1852 when ill health forced him to resign. Seven months later he died of pulmonary tuberculosis.

Power using his stethoscope

1842

ᔥ **Dr. Elisha Bartlett**, professor of theory and practice of medicine from 1844 to 1846, published one of the first worthwhile systematic discussions of typhus and typhoid fever, with detailed and accurate analysis of signs and symptoms. Like both Drs. Davidge and Potter, he disagreed with Benjamin Rush's diagnosis and treatment of patients during Philadelphia's 1793 yellow fever epidemic. Bartlett's treatise

on fevers was reproduced in four editions and earned him front rank among American physicians of his time. In 1844, while on the faculty at Maryland, he authored *An Essay on the Philosophy of Medicine*, a milestone in the development of the modern scientific method.

ᔥ **Samuel Chew**, class of 1829, was named dean.

1848

Charles Frick, class of 1845, made an initial report of chemical changes in blood resulting from disease, one of the first such reports in the country. Two years later, he published a book entitled *Renal Affections: Their Diagnosis and Pathology*. Frick became professor of materia medica and therapeutics from 1858 to 1860 and conducted exhaustive studies on the blood and urine. While performing a tracheotomy on an indigent patient, he contracted malignant diphtheria and died in 1860 at the age of 37.

In an attempt to provide a bridge between anatomy and pathology, the faculty approved a resolution making anatomical dissection compulsory, a first for U.S. medical schools (this proposal had been adopted by the trustee-controlled medical school as early as 1833, but the measure was opposed by the regent faculty at that time). Gas lamps were installed in the medical building, enabling students to conduct dissections in the evenings and avoid missing daytime lectures.

For $50, the school was shipping cadavers to medical schools as far away as Maine. The Baltimore community was becoming more tolerant of these medical school practices even though cadavers continued to be robbed from Potters Field, and there were sporadic episodes of "burking" (a term derived from Scotsman William Burke, who, during the early 1800s smothered his victims and sold their bodies to a doctor for dissection). By this time, efforts were well underway to secure passage of a law that would release unclaimed bodies to the medical school, but without success.

The last degree of bachelor of medicine was conferred. Its recipient, Rev. William O. Lumsden of Maryland, earned an MD degree the following year.

The first official convention of the newly organized American Medical Association was staged in Baltimore. The state's medical society was present at both of the preliminary planning meetings in New York and Philadelphia, and it had a large number of delegates in Baltimore.

Baltimore's Charles Street in 1848

For $50, the school was shipping cadavers to medical schools as far away as Maine.

1850

The Baltimore Infirmary was enlarged to 150 beds, making it the largest hospital in Baltimore. The expansion included a clinical amphitheater and an area for "commodious private compartments."

Maryland's school term was running from mid-October to early March, one of the longest among medical colleges. Admission to lectures and lab sessions still cost $20 for the term. The final exam cost an additional $20 each and lasted a full week at the end of the second year. Faculty examined the candidates and then conferred before casting a vote by secret ballot. A majority vote was necessary to pass; in case of a tie, a second exam became necessary.

A change in graduation requirements allowed a clinical case study to substitute for the required thesis. At the time of the school's founding in 1807, students had been required to publish a thesis, written in Latin, in order to graduate. By 1817 the "publication" requirement was dropped, and after 1824 the thesis could be written in English. Overall, a medical education at Maryland cost under $200 and brought the added benefit—unique in the nation—that a Maryland diploma automatically carried a license to practice without further examination by a state board.

An expanding Baltimore Infirmary

1852

1853

Francis Donaldson, class of 1846, after spending two years studying in European hospitals, returned to introduce the microscope to America as an essential instrument in the diagnosis of malignancy. He became the first American to advise the use of excision, aspiration and exfoliative biopsy techniques. His paper on the subject was comprehensive, with illustrations and descriptions of the microscopic appearance of cancer cells. This work long antedated that of Papanicolaou. The chair of physiology was created for him at Maryland in 1866, with hygiene and general pathology later added to the title. He held the post until 1880.

1854

&o Maryland became the first medical school in America to introduce microscopic histology in the regular curriculum. Entitled "Experimental Physiology and Microscopy," the lecture was delivered by **Christopher Johnston**, class of 1844, an accomplished physiologist and microscopist. Johnston served as professor of anatomy and physiology from 1863 to 1866 and professor of surgery from 1869 to 1881—Maryland's first graduate to hold the post. He possessed a strong interest in scientific study and research, and he was a frequent contributor to medical and surgical literature.

&o **George W. Miltenberger**, class of 1840, was named dean.

1855

Dr. George Warner Miltenberger

(Dean 1855–69)

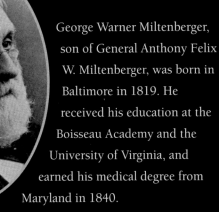

George Warner Miltenberger, son of General Anthony Felix W. Miltenberger, was born in Baltimore in 1819. He received his education at the Boisseau Academy and the University of Virginia, and earned his medical degree from Maryland in 1840.

As a student, Miltenberger attracted the attention of the faculty, and upon his graduation was selected as demonstrator of anatomy. Miltenberger taught almost every subject, providing students with broad foundations in the various branches of medicine. He was elected professor of materia medica and pathological anatomy in 1852, and served as dean of the faculty for 14 years. In 1858, he was named chair of obstetrics, gaining preeminence as a teacher and practitioner.

Miltenberger was president of both the Baltimore Obstetrical & Gynecological Society and Medical and Chirurgical Faculty, serving as chairman of the latter's library and examination committees. With the opening of the Johns Hopkins Hospital in 1889, Miltenberger was named a consulting physician.

Notorious for his dedication to work, Miltenberger did not participate in social pleasures, church services, or holidays, in order to live only for the good of his patients and his teaching. He resigned in 1891 and was made professor emeritus and honorary president of the faculty, having completed half a century of service to the medical school. Miltenberger played an instrumental role in the founding of the Medical Alumni Association in 1875.

Miltenberger's writings were published in the *Maryland Medical Journal* and in the *Transactions of the Medical and Chirurgical Faculty of Maryland*. He died in 1905. &o

1857

&o **Dr. Abram B. Arnold** reported the first three cases of scleroderma in America. A graduate of the Washington University School of Medicine in Baltimore, Arnold served as professor of clinical medicine and diseases of the nervous system from 1872 to 1880. Earlier, in 1855, he authored *A Manual of Nervous Diseases*.

University of Maryland

SIXTY-FIFTH ANNUAL CIRCULAR

OF THE

School of Medicine,

N. E. Cor. Lombard and Green Streets, Baltimore, Md.

SESSION 1872-73.

Baltimore:
PRINTED BY KELLY, PIET & COMPANY,
PRINTERS, BOOKSELLERS AND STATIONERS, 174 BALTIMORE ST.

Chapter Three

1860~1890

Civil War

1860

Prior to the outbreak of the Civil War, there was one physician in Maryland for every 628 people, one of the country's highest ratios. With rather modest incomes from fees collected, doctors often found themselves working as farmers, merchants, politicians, writers, or members of the clergy.

At the medical school, the number of students with prior college experience had reached a record 35 percent, up from 10 percent in 1825. But officials feared that the commencement of a civil war would ruin the medical school, as it continued to rely on enrollment fees for its survival. The fallout was not as great as expected.

Maryland's Enrollment Figures During the Civil War		
Year	Students	Graduates
1860–61	150	63
1861–62	114	52
1862–63	103	37
1863–64	130	56
1864–65	163	58

Among the members of the class of 1860, roughly 30 percent fought for the Confederacy, while about 10 percent fought for the Union. The medical school capitalized on the war, instituting a popular course in military surgery and offering hospital facilities to the government for $5 per week for each hospitalized soldier, a price $2 higher than that asked of private patients.

TEXT BOOKS.

The Faculty recommend the following text books:

ANATOMY AND PHYSIOLOGY—Quain and Sharpey, Wilson's Anatomy, Carpenter's Elements, Kirkes and Paget's Physiology.

SURGERY—Druitt's Surgery, Pirrie's Surgery, Erichsen's Surgery.

CHEMISTRY AND PHARMACY—Turner's Chemistry, Fowne's Chemistry, Graham's Chemistry, Bowman's Medical Chemistry, Parrish's Practical Pharmacy.

OBSTETRICS AND DISEASES OF WOMEN AND CHILDREN—Cazeaux's, Churchill's, Rigby's Midwifery; West's, Evanson's, Condie's Diseases of Children.

PRINCIPLES AND PRACTICE OF MEDICINE—Watson's Lectures, Williams on Diseases of the Chest, Latham on the Heart, Barlow's Practice of Medicine.

MATERIA MEDICA, THERAPEUTICS AND PATHOLOGY—Pereira's Materia Medica, Wood and Bache's Dispensatory, Vogel's and Gross's Pathological Anatomy.

Citizens of Baltimore baracade the streets for the invasion of Maryland.

1862

⧉ **Dr. William Alexander Hammond**, professor of anatomy and physiology for the 1860–61 school year, was named surgeon general of the U.S. Army during the Civil War, a post he held until 1864. Hammond organized a system for evacuating wounded soldiers from the battlefield. He developed the military hospital and medical system, the first in the world. In addition, his methods of maintaining military records, reports, and compiling data was hailed as an enormous contribution to medical science and later, to medical history. He also created the Army Medical Museum, later renamed the Armed Forces Institute of Pathology.

During Hammond's brief tenure at Maryland, he presented the lectureship on experimental physiology and microscopy. Microscopes were provided in the school's museum to create one of America's largest microscopic collections. Specimens of all the tissues and structures comprising the entire body were available for viewing by students round-the-clock. The faculty took great pride in introducing the nation to this method of histologic study.

He [Hammond] developed the military hospital and medical system, the first in the world.

Civil War

1865

 Samuel A. Mudd, class of 1856, treated John Wilkes Booth for a fracture of the tibia sustained when Booth jumped from the presidential box at Ford's Theater after assassinating U.S. President Abraham Lincoln. Mudd was later convicted of aiding, abetting and assisting the Lincoln conspirators and received a life sentence at Fort Jefferson, Florida. Four years later, he received a pardon from President Andrew Johnson for his heroic effort in caring for prisoners and guards during a yellow fever epidemic. Mudd died of pneumonia in 1883.

 Radical change came to Maryland's curriculum following the Civil War: most noticeably an increased emphasis on specialties and considerably more clinical teaching. Baltimore experienced an influx of talented new physicians. The majority migrated from the South, but a few had trained abroad during the war and now offered more advanced qualifications.

To support this new wave of specialization, Maryland revised its courses to include intensive introductions to neurology, ophthalmology, throat and chest diseases and various branches of surgery. The first clinics on eye disease were organized, as well as lectures on the physiology and pathology of the kidney, complete with a demonstration of chemical and microscopic urinalysis.

Many of these specialists were invited to take positions as adjunct faculty. An optional ten-week summer session of special studies and specialized dispensary opportunities were offered. The increase in clinical teaching would serve as a bridge between the old apprenticeship system and modern internship/residency training. Students were required to spend at least three hours each day in various clinics. By 1869, Maryland would graduate 83 students in a single class.

Alumni gathering at a medical meeting include Riggin Buckler (1853), Charles O'Donovan (1853), Samuel C. Chew (1858), W. Van Bibber (1845), Allen Smith (1861), Christopher Johnston (1844), Francis Donaldson (1846), Joseph A. Steuart (1850), Thomas Murdoch (1850), and Ferdinand E. Chatard (1861)

1867

Maryland established the nation's first chair of diseases of women and children (gynecology and pediatrics), appointing **William T. Howard** to the post. Educated at Jefferson Medical College in Philadelphia, Howard settled in North Carolina where he practiced until the end of the war. His first appointment at Maryland was as lecturer on auscultation and percussion during Maryland's summer session in 1866. In 1884, Howard was elected president of the American Gynecological Association, an organization he helped establish.

Alan Penniman Smith, class of 1861, was named an incorporator of the Johns Hopkins University, which opened in 1876. The son of Nathan Ryno Smith, the younger Smith was a capable surgeon whose neighbor and friend was wealthy merchant and industrialist Johns Hopkins. Hopkins had earlier named Smith to be a trustee of his proposed hospital, which opened in 1889. From 1868 to 1870, Smith served as an adjunct professor of surgery at Maryland.

Members of Class of 1869

1869

1868

The Maryland General Assembly appropriated $2,500 annually to Maryland for providing continuous free service to one patient from each county and legislative district, as well as free tuition to one student from each county and district. In addition, the Infirmary instituted an afternoon out-patient program, providing free medications and consultations to the community. The $4,000 per year income received by the clinical program from the city for operations proved insufficient and forced the university further into debt. The blame first fell on the Sisters of Charity who provided nursing care. They were accused of wastefulness, but when the university tried to hire private nurses, the debt increased. The Sisters of Mercy were recruited to reduce the deficit, and additional cuts followed in the budgets for salaries and teaching equipment.

William Maxwell Wood, class of 1829, became the first surgeon general of the U.S. Navy. The appointment by President Ulysses Grant came at the height of Wood's distinguished 40-year career in the Navy which included serving as fleet surgeon for a number of squadrons. But he is best remembered for his journey through Mexico behind enemy lines at the outset of the war  with Mexico, when he was instrumental in conveying intelligence to the Pacific Squadron that enabled the U.S. to take control of California. Wood served as physician to U.S. president Zachary Taylor, and later had two destroyers named in his honor: the *USS Wood* from 1919 to 1930; and the *USS William M. Wood* from 1945 to 1976.

Dr. Julian John Chisolm

(Dean 1869–74)

Julian John Chisolm was born in Charleston, South Carolina, in 1830. He earned his medical degree from the Medical College of South Carolina in 1850 and studied in London and Paris. He was professor of surgery at the Medical College of South Carolina from 1858 to 1868 and during the Civil War treated the first wounded soldiers at Fort Sumter. He was regarded as one of the most famous surgeons in the Confederate Army. Chisolm joined Maryland's faculty in 1868, becoming professor of operative surgery and clinical professor of diseases of the eye and ear. He served as dean of faculty until 1874. In 1873, he relinquished his chair of operative surgery when the department of eye and ear diseases was elevated to equal status as the other chairs in the faculty.

Chisolm served as president of nearly every national and international ophthalmological society of his day. He was founder and chief surgeon of the Presbyterian Eye, Ear and Throat Hospital in Baltimore, chairman of the ophthalmological section of the International Medical Congress, and president of the Baltimore Academy of Medicine. The author of several editions of the *Manual of Military Surgery*, Chisolm is recognized for performing the first outpatient surgery for cataracts in America.

Chisolm was considered a leader among the third generation of medical school professors, and is credited with helping to guide American medicine toward specialization. He died in 1903. ∾

Maryland faculty members Drs. Francis T. Miles (seated left) and Julian Chisholm (seated right)

1869

∾ **Dr. Julian J. Chisolm** was named dean.

∾ **Dr. Francis T. Miles** became the first physician in Maryland to teach the subject of nervous diseases as a specialty. While serving as professor of anatomy from 1869 to 1880, the clinical department of nervous diseases was added to his position. Later, from 1880 to 1883, Miles was professor of physiology. His research contributions centered on the subjects of cerebral tumor, methods of localization, the importance of counter-irritation, and the use of galvanic current. He was president of the American Neurological Association from 1880 to 1882. He wrote "Diseases of the Peripheral Nerves" in Pepper's *System of Practical Medicine, Regional Diagnosis in Brain Disease* (1877), and *Electricity in Medicine* (1878). Miles earned his medical degree in 1849 from the Medical College of South Carolina and later served as a member of its faculty. During the Civil War, he joined the Confederacy as an infantry captain and was wounded during one of the battles around Charleston. At one point he acted as major and was in charge of Fort Sumter during the assault by the Federal fleet.

1872

≈ **Aaron Friedenwald**, class of 1860, was the first to report in the American literature the von Graefe method of iridectomy for treatment of glaucoma. An office student of Dr. Nathan Smith, Friedenwald served as professor of diseases of the eye and ear from 1873 to 1902. In 1890, Friedenwald was instrumental in the founding of the Association of American Medical Colleges, serving as its first vice president and later president. The organization was created to improve the nation's health by enhancing the effectiveness of academic medicine. Later, in 1897, he published an important literary contribution, *The History of Jewish Physicians*.

1874

≈ **Samuel C. Chew**, class of 1858, was named dean.

Dr. Samuel Claggett Chew
(Dean 1874–79)

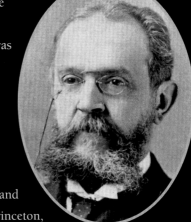

Born in Baltimore in 1837, Samuel Claggett Chew was the son of Dr. Samuel Chew, dean of the faculty at the medical school from 1842 to 1844.

He earned AB and AM degrees at Princeton, and studied medicine under the direction of his father. Chew was awarded a medical degree from Maryland in 1858. In 1864, after the death of his father, Chew was elected professor of materia medica and practice, and his deanship spanned the years 1874 through 1879. Chew became professor of the principles and practice of medicine in 1886, a position he held for 24 years. It is estimated that he taught nearly 4,000 students during his tenure at Maryland.

A member of the medical faculty for more than 40 years, Chew played a prominent role in both the material and educational life of the university, and he was known as a leading influence on school policy. He was also recognized as one of Baltimore's most distinguished medical professionals.

Chew served the Medical Alumni Association and the Medical and Chirurgical Faculty of Maryland in various capacities. He was president of the board of trustees of the Peabody Institute, a consulting physician to the Johns Hopkins Hospital, and one of the authors of Pepper's *System of Practical Medicine*. Chew died in 1915. ≈

1874

℘ **Roberts Bartholow**, class of 1852, confirmed that electrical stimulation of the human cortex on one side stimulates the muscles on the opposite side of the body. Bartholow used as his subject a servant of his household who had advanced cancer of the scalp. Upon publication of this highly controversial experiment, Bartholow was forced to leave his academic post in Cincinnati. Earlier, in 1863, he authored the Army's manual on conducting physical examinations of draftees and recruits. He was commissioned to produce the document by William Hammond, Surgeon General of the U.S. Army and former Maryland faculty member. Bartholow later authored *Materia Medica and Therapeutics*, which advanced through 11 editions; and *The Treatise on the Practice of Medicine*, which went through five editions.

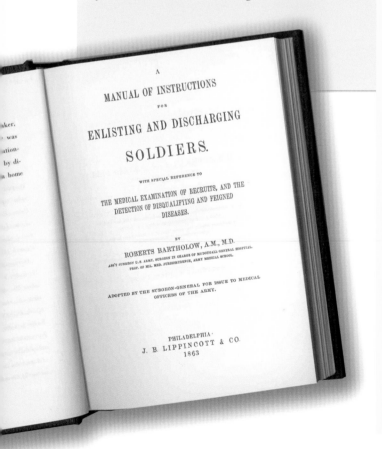

A

MANUAL OF INSTRUCTIONS

FOR

ENLISTING AND DISCHARGING

SOLDIERS.

WITH SPECIAL REFERENCE TO

THE MEDICAL EXAMINATION OF RECRUITS, AND THE
DETECTION OF DISQUALIFYING AND FEIGNED
DISEASES.

BY

ROBERTS BARTHOLOW, A.M., M.D.

ASS'T SURGEON U.S. ARMY, SURGEON IN CHARGE OF MCDOUGALL GENERAL HOSPITAL.
PROF. OF MIL. MED. JURISPRUDENCE, ARMY MEDICAL SCHOOL.

ADOPTED BY THE SURGEON-GENERAL FOR ISSUE TO MEDICAL
OFFICERS OF THE ARMY.

PHILADELPHIA:
J. B. LIPPINCOTT & CO.
1863

"$\mathcal{M}$*uch may be done by an active and influential association, both through moral influences and substantial support, to stimulate, encourage and strengthen the efforts of those who for the time being direct and control the destinies of the institution."*

~*Eugene F. Cordell, Class of 1868*

1875

℘ The school's medical alumni association was founded with the election of **Robert E. Dorsey**, class of 1819, as president. Efforts to establish the association started one year earlier, during commencement exercises at Ford's Opera House. Leading the effort was George W. Miltenberger, class of 1840. The former dean created the framework for a free-standing alumni association, supported

entirely by financial contributions from its membership and immune to the ebbs and flows of institutional funding. Another organizer, **Richard S. Steuart**, class of 1822, served as chairman during the year of planning.

Dr. Richard S. Steuart

℘ As a result of a $30,000 appropriation by the state in 1873, a Greene Street wing was completed and added to the Infirmary. It was three stories high with a basement. The addition greatly increased the clinical facilities of the university, as the hospital now had double the capacity of any similar institution in Baltimore. Included was a new lying-in department, and the department for diseases of children was also established by the transfer of patients from St. Andrew's home. The expansion allowed the hospital to handle 1,200 patients a year.

1877

ॐ **Thomas A. Ashby**, class of 1873, established the *Maryland Medical Journal* and served as its editor. Five years later, in 1882, Ashby helped found The Women's Medical College of Baltimore. He was its chair of obstetrics and gynecology until 1897 when he became professor of diseases of women at Maryland, a position he held until his death in 1916. In addition to his medical duties, Ashby was elected to the Maryland House of Delegates and served one term beginning in 1912.

1878

ॐ **George H. Rohe**, class of 1873, produced a treatise on leprosy in Baltimore. The first report of this ancient disease in Maryland included actual reports of three cases observed during ten years. Rohe was professor of clinical dermatology and hygiene at the College of Physicians and Surgeons from 1878 to 1880. He made significant contributions in the field of dermatology, particularly with respect to herpetic infections and venereal diseases.

1879

ॐ **W. J. McDowell**, class of 1871, presented a paper to the Medical and Chirurgical Faculty of Maryland on the use of sodium salicylate for treatment of rheumatic iridocyclitis, the first use of this agent in ophthalmologic practice. McDowell became assistant surgeon of the Presbyterian Eye and Ear Charity Hospital and the Baltimore Eye and Ear Infirmary.

ॐ **Louis M. Tiffany**, class of 1868, was named dean.

On left, the Greene Street addition to the infirmary.

Dr. Louis McLane Tiffany

(Dean 1879–86)

Louis McLane Tiffany was born in Baltimore in 1844. He received AB and AM degrees from the University of Cambridge, England, prior to receiving his medical degree from Maryland in 1868.

A resident physician at the Baltimore Almshouse, Tiffany served in various capacities at Maryland. He was demonstrator in anatomy, professor of operative surgery, professor of surgery, and dean of the faculty from 1879 to 1886. During his demonstratorship, he served as chair of anatomy for the Maryland Dental College. Tiffany held many leadership positions in the medical community, including president of the Baltimore Medical Association, president of the Clinical Society of Maryland, vice president and president of the Medical and Chirurgical Faculty, and surgeon-in-chief for the Baltimore and Ohio Railroad.

A skillful and innovative surgeon whose studious, patient, and conservative nature was balanced by his bold and self-confident approach, Tiffany made important contributions to surgery of the kidney and maxilla. In 1878, he performed a temporary depression of each maxilla for angiosarcoma of both nares, preceded by tracheotomy, a procedure lauded as "the most difficult and heroic operation recorded in the annals of surgery." This accomplishment attracted national attention, and in 1855 Tiffany reported the first successful nephrolithotomy in America. He was the first surgeon to use a pearl button to anchor stay sutures after abdominal surgery.

Tiffany served as president of the American Surgical Association and the Southern Surgical and Gynecological Association. An avid sportsman and athlete, he particularly enjoyed hunting, and fishing. Tiffany died in Virginia in 1916. ഇ

1879

ഇ **James M. M. Ambler**, class of 1870, a surgeon in the U.S. Navy, volunteered for the *Jeanette* Polar Expedition, one of the few attempts to enter the Arctic Ocean via the Behring Strait. The *Jeannette* set sail from San Francisco on July 8. But on September 6, days after passing the Behring Strait, the ship was frozen in the ice. For nearly two years the ice pack drifted, carrying the ship with it. The *Jeannette* sank on June 12, 1881, crushed by ice. Lifeboats, sleds, and provisions were salvaged, and the crew began searching for safety over ice and water. In September, the three surviving boats were separated by a fierce gale of wind and only one was rescued. The second was never heard from again. The crew on the third, which included Ambler and lieutenant commander George W. DeLong, survived until late October when all died of starvation. Ambler's log survived, recording his treatment of patients until the day of his death.

The Jeannette *set sail from San Francisco on July 8. But on September 6, days after passing the Behring Strait, the ship was frozen in the ice. For nearly two years the ice pack drifted, carrying the ship with it. The* Jeannette *sank on June 12, 1881, crushed by ice.*

1880

✂ Samuel Theobald, class of 1867, became the first physician to report boric acid as a useful remedy in the treatment of eye disease. Following graduation, Theobald studied ophthalmology at the Royal London Hospital and with Adam Politzer in Vienna. He published *Prevalent Diseases of the Eye* in 1906, a textbook complete with helpful suggestions for both the general practitioner and the ophthalmologist. Theobald served on the faculty of Johns Hopkins from 1894 to 1930. Perhaps his most noted advancement was his method of treating closure of the tear ducts and in Theobald's *Lachrymal Probes*.

✂ Eugene Cordell, class of 1868, published a paper on erysipelatous pneumonia, a rare lung infection, the first report on this disorder in America. Cordell was professor of materia medica and therapeutics at the Women's Medical College in Baltimore. He was named honorary professor of the history of medicine at Maryland and made a lasting contribution to the medical school and hospital through his studious and painstaking publications dealing with Maryland graduates and faculty members. His books on the medical annals of Maryland are priceless historical resources.

The earliest known photograph of Davidge Hall, circa 1880

1881

✂ J. Ford Thompson, class of 1857, one of the best known surgeons in Washington, D.C., was consulted when U.S. President James A. Garfield was shot on July 2. Mortally wounded, Garfield was treated in the White House for weeks. Inventor Alexander Graham Bell tried unsuccessfully to find the bullet with a specially designed device. On September 6, Garfield was taken to the New Jersey seaside. For a few days he seemed to be recuperating, but on September 19, 1881, he died from an infection and internal hemorrhage. Thompson also served as family physician for a number of U.S. cabinet members.

1882

ℝ The Maryland General Assembly passed a supplementary measure to the act of 1812 which created the University of Maryland. It authorized the regents to grant degrees, diplomas and certificates to students of dental surgery, pharmacy and other "cognate branches of medical science in the university."

ℝ During a shortage of bodies for dissection, the Maryland General Assembly passed the "Anatomy Law." The act permitted physicians to take possession of bodies of indigents scheduled for burial at the public's expense for use "within the state for the advancement of medical science." The legislation was also intended to end the practices of grave robbing and "burking" in Maryland.

The act permitted physicians to take possession of bodies of indigents scheduled for burial at the public's expense for use "within the state for the advancement of medical science."

1883

➷ **Newberry A. S. Keyser**, class of 1883, while a medical student, published a convincing paper confirming Neisser's observations of 1879 and 1882 that the gonococcus causes gonorrhea. He also showed that Ehrlich's use of methylene blue as a stain, reported in 1881, was a reliable technique. Keyser's bacteriological knowledge and investigative evidence antedated that of Dr. William Welch, a recognized authority in Baltimore and in America.

1884

➷ **Dr. Randolph Winslow**, professor of surgery and chairman of the department of surgery from 1902 to 1920, was the first surgeon in Maryland to shorten uterine ligaments. He helped found the Association of American Medical Colleges, was a founder of the American College of Surgeons, and served as president of the Southern Surgical Association. Dr. Winslow was one of the first advocates of aseptic surgery and became the first surgeon in Maryland to perform a pyloric resection for cancer in 1885, the first vaginal hysterectomy in 1888, and to operate successfully for gunshot wounds of the intestine in 1893.

Dr. Randolph Winslow

1886

➷ **Jacob E. Michael**, class of 1873, was named dean.

Dr. Jacob Edwin Michael
(Dean 1886–89, 1893–96)

Jacob Edwin Michael was born in Harford County, Maryland, in 1848. He was educated at St. Timothy's Hall in Catonsville and the Newark Academy in Delaware. Michael received an AB degree from Princeton in 1871 and a medical degree from Maryland in 1873. A man of tremendous stature and strength, Michael was a distinguished athlete during his years at Princeton.

Michael joined Maryland's faculty in 1874, serving as demonstrator of anatomy for the next six years. He was professor of anatomy, professor of obstetrics, and dean of the faculty from 1886 to 1889 and from 1893 to 1896. In 1884, he was appointed professor of genitourinary and rectal surgery at Baltimore Polyclinic. A skillful surgeon and a popular teacher, Michael was noted for his speaking abilities. While firm in his opinions, he was considered liberal and tolerant.

In addition to serving as editor of the *Maryland Medical Journal*, Michael held various leadership positions in the local medical community. He was president of the Clinical Society and the Baltimore Medical Association, vice president and president of the Medical and Chirurgical Faculty, and president of the Medical Alumni Association.

Michael died at age 47 after a two-year struggle with Bright's Disease. ➷

*T*he medical school assisted in the passage of the Lunacy Bill, making the state responsible for "just and humane" treatment of the insane, and providing for a lunacy commission to supervise public, private, and corporate institutions treating the insane.

1886

❧ The last known case of "burking" in Baltimore is recorded. Emily Brown was murdered in Pig Alley. Her body was placed in a sack and delivered to the medical school. Maryland's janitor, Perry, took possession of the body and paid the murderer, Ross, and his accomplice $5 each. Ross was arrested, convicted, and hanged at the city jail, while both Perry and the accomplice fled. Later, upon his death, Perry's body was sent to the medical school for dissection, but it was rendered useless when a fire obliterated the building storing cadavers.

1888

❧ **Leonard E. Neale**, class of 1881, invented an axis traction forceps, combining some of the useful features of the Simpson and Tarnier instruments. Neale was professor of obstetrics at the College of Physicians and Surgeons and held the same position at Maryland in 1896. He studied in European clinics and was regarded as the best qualified obstetrical teacher and practitioner in Baltimore.

1887

❧ A free, lying-in hospital for expectant mothers opened near campus. It was made possible through an annual $2,500 state appropriation and was placed under the direction of Maryland's professor and demonstrator of obstetrics and two resident physicians. Its 24 beds handled 308 cases in its first three years of operation. Students were encouraged to visit the facility to gain valuable experience during their final year of classes.

Councilman published a monograph on the etiology and pathology of variola and vaccinia, acknowledged to be a classic in the field.

1889

℘ The Maryland Training School for nurses opened at the infirmary under the direction of **Louisa Parsons**, an 1860 graduate of the Miss Nightingale's Nursing School and Home. The school was established as a solution to the shortage of hospital labor and consisted of a two-year apprenticeship. The name was later changed to the University of Maryland School of Nursing.

Drs. William Councilman and William H. Welch at Cleveland-Western Reserve University for the dedication of the Institute of Pathology in 1929

1890

so **William T. Councilman**, class of 1878, made his initial report of the hepatic manifestations in patients with yellow fever and his description of an acidophilic body later known as *Councilman Body*. Councilman was Dr. William Welch's first resident at City Hospital and a faculty member in physiology, anatomy and pathology at Johns Hopkins. He taught classes in pathology at both Maryland and the College of Physicians and Surgeons from 1883 to 1886. In 1892, he was selected as the Shattuck Professor of Anatomy at the Harvard Medical School. Twelve years later he published a monograph on the etiology and pathology of variola and vaccinia, acknowledged to be a classic in the field. His studies—made with various associates—on meningitis (demonstration of the meningococcus as a causative agent) were also significant contributions.

so **Isaac E. Atkinson**, class of 1865, was named dean.

Dr. Isaac Edmundson Atkinson
(Dean 1890–93)

Isaac Edmondson Atkinson was born in Baltimore in 1846. He received a medical degree from Maryland in 1865 at the age of 19.

During a smallpox epidemic in Baltimore, Atkinson was made superintendent of vaccination. He, two classmates and 11 others were founders of the American Dermatological Association in 1876. Atkinson served as clinical professor of dermatology at Maryland from 1879 to 1881, professor of pathology from 1881 to 1886, professor of materia medica and therapeutics from 1886 to 1900, and emeritus professor. He was dean of the faculty from 1890 to 1893.

The operator of a large consulting practice, Atkinson was highly regarded for the depth of his medical knowledge, diagnostic powers, and excellent judgment. His primary focus was on general medicine, although he had keen interest in syphilis and diseases of the skin.

Atkinson was author of a section in Pepper's *System of Practical Medicine* and published several journal articles. A consulting physician at the Johns Hopkins Hospital and a member of the Lunacy Commission of Maryland, Atkinson was president of the Clinical Society of Maryland, vice president and president of the Medical and Chirurgical Faculty and president of the American Dermatological Society. He died of pneumonia in 1906. so

WAR DEPARTMENT,
SURGEON GENERAL'S OFFICE
LIBRARY
WASHINGTON.

Sept. 7. 1900
1.15 P. M.

My dear Carroll:

Hip! Hip! Hip! Hurrah! God be praised for the news from Cuba today — Carroll much improved — Prognosis very good". I still

Chapter Four

1891~1906

*M*aryland was on stable financial footing. Other than a $200 ground rental fee for a portion of the infirmary lot, the hospital was debt free. The balance owed on the Lying-in Hospital was insignificant, and debt had been retired on the dental buildings. As long as students showed up for classes and paid their fees, the institution would be fine.

Medical schools were popping up everywhere. There were now 157 in America, including seven in Maryland. Medical degrees were awarded to 455 students in the state during the prior year, including 111 from the institution located on Lombard and Greene streets.

This fierce competition for students led many institutions to lower their academic standards. Critics argued that most were proprietary schools more interested in profit than education. Maryland was caught in the downdraft. Requirements like its graduation thesis—mandatory since the school's founding in 1807—had been eliminated at the conclusion of the 1886-87 session.

America was graduating more doctors, but without proper oversight the quality of medical care was going to suffer. The National Association of Medical Colleges decided to take charge. It announced a set of admissions requirements and education programs that would become the standard for all medical schools. The changes would coincide with the establishment of state examining boards charged with upholding a rigid system of requirements for those entering the practice of medicine.

Under the new standards, medical school applicants would be required to present either a diploma from a respectable college or high school, a teacher's certificate, or to pass a written examination in English. A three-year curriculum would be mandatory, featuring four courses per year, each concluding with a written examination.

These new standards would be a stretch for Maryland. Officials worried that upgrading the minimum requirements would result in a sharp reduction in enrollment, threatening the school's solvency. Some, according to Cordell, "declared that the step was a suicidal one."

1891

These new standards would be a stretch for Maryland. Officials worried that upgrading the minimum requirements would result in a sharp reduction in enrollment, threatening the school's solvency. Some, according to Cordell, "declared that the step was a suicidal one."

Maryland's problem was its lack of endowment. "The scientific requirements of modern medicine," Cordell wrote, "demand a large outlay which cannot be met by the mere fees of students, fluctuating and hence uncertain as they necessarily are."

Cordell urged the school to take a more aggressive role in fund raising. He identified two primary constituencies: faculty, because "they owe so much of their reputation and success to the opportunities and incentives which their positions in the institution have afforded;" and alumni "because of the hallowed ties that bind them to the 'dear mother' and because they must share with her her honor or dishonor, her reputation or infamy."

The faculty accepted the new standards. More would follow. In 1895, the Association was calling for a fourth year of study, and Maryland again had no choice but to comply despite witnessing a 50 percent drop in its number of graduates.

And just down the road would come the Flexner Report. Released in 1910, it was the most significant event in the evolution of medical education in America. Commissioned by the Carnegie Foundation, the report criticized proprietary schools and lobbied for schools that mimicked those operating under the German system.

This model blended strong biomedical sciences with hands-on clinical training. As a result, many schools closed while others were forced into mergers.

It would be a bumpy road for the institution, but officials were determined to persevere. Over the next 15 years, Practice Hall received a $4,000 remodeling effort. But the structure, located beside the medical building, burned down in December 1893 and required another $8,000 to rebuild. Flames had also reached the old medical building but were quickly extinguished. In fact, between 1891 and 1907, the university acquired nearly a dozen buildings for its growing campus, but as time wore on it could no longer afford to paint them.

1892

1893

ⅆ **Samuel T. Earle**, class of 1870, was named president of the first Maryland State Board of Medical Examiners. Earle's specialty was proctology, and he served on the faculty of the Baltimore Medical College from 1896 to 1907.

ⅆ **James R. Brown**, class of 1875, the first head of the genitourinary clinic and the Johns Hopkins Hospital, became the first physician to catheterize the male ureter. The procedure was performed at its outpatient clinic. It is regarded as a pioneering procedure in the diagnosis and treatment of diseases of the kidney. Brown died two years later of tuberculosis.

ⅆ One way to reduce an institution's dependence on revenues from tuition was to build an endowment-large sums of money that generate income each year to help cover the school's operating expenses. In an attempt to bolster fund raising, the Medical Alumni Association Board of Directors established The Trustees of the Endowment of the University of Maryland, Inc., a subsidiary group responsible for investing endowment gifts to benefit the medical school. Organizers included alumni Jacob Michael, Samuel C. Chew and Eugene Cordell.

Faculty of Physic, University of Maryland 1893.

1894

so **Dr. Thomas C. Gilchrist** described the first case of Blastomycosis of the skin. His significant contribution was the identification and isolation of the double-contoured spore Blastomyces dermatitidis. He identified the organisms under the microscope and made accurate drawings of great value. Gilchrist held dual appointments as clinical professor of dermatology at Maryland and Johns Hopkins.

so **Sylvan H. Likes**, class of 1893, advocated the use of prophylactics against venereal disease. Powerful influences and agencies in both professional and lay circles in Baltimore argued that Likes' ideas would encourage vice and immorality. Rather than provoke further criticism, Likes did not attempt to openly popularize his ideas and thus failed to receive the national recognition he justly deserved.

Dr. Thomas C. Gilchrist

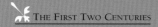

1896

U of M, 5   JHU, 0

A football team, consisting of medical, law, and dental students was formed by medical student Norfleet Gibbs, class of 1896. The movement was the university's first attempt to bring together students from these three units on campus. It sparked formation of a University of Maryland Athletic Association in 1896, guided by a faculty/student executive committee. Within a few years, baseball, ice hockey, track, tennis, and basketball teams were organized and competed against the Maryland State College of Agriculture, St. John's College, Navy, Georgetown, Johns Hopkins, and occasionally Rutgers and North Carolina.

The school colors of maroon and black were established around 1890 by dental student William Oakley Haines. He was preparing a specimen plate (set of teeth) for graduation. Looking for something to set his work apart from that of classmates, he selected maroon and black as the kinds of rubber to use. A dental supply vendor passed by and asked Haines if he could tell him the colors of the school. The student was about to reply "we haven't any," but instead was struck with the idea that perhaps the shades of rubber in his plate would make nice colors; so he answered "maroon and black." The next day, the vendor appeared with twenty yards of maroon and black ribbon wrapped about his arm and cried "Here are your college colors, only five cents." A short time later the colors were

adopted during a meeting of the three departments in Anatomical Hall.

With the merger of Maryland and the State College of Agriculture in 1920, organized athletics moved to College Park. New colors were adopted, and sporting activities on the Baltimore campus were reduced to club sports.

Dr. Robert Dorsey Coale

(Dean 1896–97, 1900–15)

Born in Baltimore in 1857, Robert Dorsey Coale was the great-grandson of Dr. Samuel Stringer Coale, a prominent figure in early Baltimore medical circles. His maternal grandfather was Dr. Robert Edward Dorsey, a Maryland alumnus, reputable physician, and professor of materia medica in the faculty of the trustees.

Coale graduated from the Pennsylvania Military Academy in 1875 and earned a PhD degree from the Johns Hopkins University in 1882, six years after he enjoyed the distinction of becoming the very first matriculant accepted at that institution.

Coale became professor of toxicology and chemistry at Maryland, serving two terms as dean for a total of 18 years. An executive of sound, conservative judgment, and an individual of unswerving integrity, Coale was, to a large extent, the balance wheel of the faculty. Although kindly and generous to a fault, he was a man of few words, a trait many mistook for coldness. Virtually all his charity was done anonymously.

A military man as well as a scientist, he was frequently addressed as Colonel Coale. He served as a colonel in the 5th Maryland U.S. Volunteers during the Spanish-American War. When he died at his desk in 1915, a handful of due bills were found in his safe. They represented money he had loaned to students in need. It is said that the students had lost their greatest friend and most ardent champion. ∾

Simon is remembered as a pioneer American virologist.

1896

∾ **Dr. Robert D. Coale** was named dean.

∾ The Hospital for Crippled and Deformed Children became affiliated with Maryland. The hospital was later named the James Lawrence Kernan Hospital and Industrial School of Maryland for Crippled Children.

∾ **Charles E. Simon**, class of 1890, published *Manual of Clinical Diagnosis*, which went through 10 editions and became a standard textbook for medical schools throughout the country. Early in his career, Simon was recognized for his work in the field of gastroenterology, and he was one of the founding members of the American Gastroenterological Association in 1897. He joined Maryland's faculty in 1915 as professor of clinical pathology & experimental medicine and later became professor of physiological chemistry & clinical pathology. Educated in Germany, Simon's pro-German political beliefs caused problems for him with his colleagues at the onset of World War I, and in 1919 Simon resigned his position. He joined the staff at the Johns Hopkins School of Hygiene and Public Health where he became professor of filterable viruses, and he was responsible for developing virology as an independent area of medical research. Simon is remembered as a pioneer American virologist.

1897

∾ **Charles W. Mitchell**, class of 1881, was named dean.

Dr. Charles Wellman Mitchell

(Dean 1897–1900)

Charles Wellman Mitchell was born in Baltimore in 1859. He earned a BA degree at Princeton in 1879, and later an AM degree at the same institution. Mitchell received his medical degree and examination medal from Maryland in 1881.

A lecturer in pathology at Maryland, and professor of the diseases of children at the Women's Medical College, Mitchell's interest in pathology was stimulated by his study in Vienna. His expertise in pathogenesis attracted the best students to the medical school. Mitchell became professor of clinical medicine at Maryland in 1893 and professor of materia medica in 1896. He was elected professor of the diseases of children in 1897, and served as dean of the faculty from 1897 to 1900. It was during his deanship that the first class required to fulfill a four-year curriculum graduated. Mitchell was president of the Maryland Medical Society and a visiting physician at the Union Protestant Infirmary.

When Mitchell died in 1917, he was remembered as an excellent teacher who instinctively understood his students. ℘

1897

℘ A new hospital building opened on the site of the old Infirmary. It consisted of five stories and 190 beds and was funded by $20,000 in public contributions and $70,000 in bonds sold by the professors. The name of the hospital was changed from the Baltimore Infirmary to University Hospital.

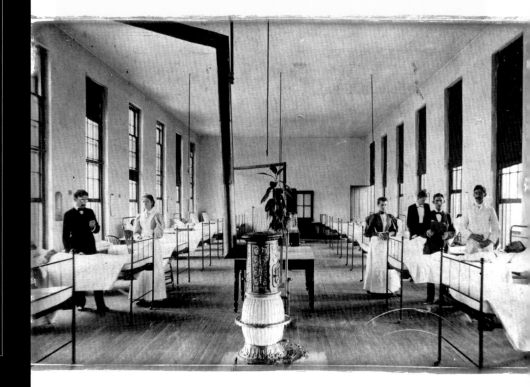

The campus before the turn of the century

1904

Dr. Edward N.
Brush, professor of psy-
chiatry at Maryland, was
named editor of *American
Journal of Insanity* (later
known as the *American
Journal of Psychiatry*). He
served in this capacity until
1931. Sought after in
medico-legal work, Brush
was an expert witness in
the Schneider Case where,
for the first time in the
U.S., the experts sum-
moned by both the plaintiff
and the defendant met
together and correlated
their findings to present to
the judge.

The medical school
received its first direct
appropriation from the
state legislature, a total of
$5,000.

Baltimore Street east of Hanover Street, before the 1904 fire

1904

On February 7, an explosion at the Hurst Company Building, located between Hopkins Place and Liberty Street, set off a two-day fire in the city. The flames raced through 86 streets in the downtown, destroying 1,500 buildings and 2,500 businesses. The medical building and entire University of Maryland campus survived the *Great Baltimore Fire of 1904*.

1905

EXTRA **THE**

VOLUME CXXXIV—NO. 84.   BALTIMORE, MON

TWENTY-FOUR BLO

IN HEART

CITY'S MOST VALUABLE

LOSS VARIOUSLY ESTI

FROM $50,00

BLAZE STILL SPREADING EASTWARD

Starting In John E. Hurst Build
To Lombard, East To Holliday
Destroying Wholesale Bus
Continental, Equitable, Ca
tral, The Sun And Othe

Personal and Prompt Attention
To Repairing Heating Plants
In Partially Wrecked Buildings.
Reasonable Prices Charged.
ALVA HUBBARD HEATING COMPANY,
420 North Calvert street.

THE SUN TODAY.

This edition of The Sun is printed from the presses of the Washington Star, through the courtesy of that paper. When the great fire was close to The Sun Building, in Baltimore, a force of editors, reporters, compositors and stereotypers was sent to Washington and duplicate news facilities were installed in the Star office.

SUMMARY OF THE NEWS.

Government Weather Report.
Washington, Feb. 7.—The Government Weather Bureau issued the following forecast for Monday and Tuesday:
Maryland, District of Columbia, Virginia, Delaware and Eastern Pennsylvania, fair, much colder Monday; cold wave at night; brisk to high northwest winds; Tuesday fair and cold.
West Virginia, fair Monday, except snow in the mountain districts, cold wave; Tuesday fair and cold.
North Carolina, fair and colder Monday, cold wave at night in the interior; Tuesday fair and

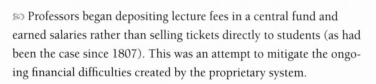

around the bank building was blazing, it did not catch fire until 7 o'clock and was only partially destroyed.

Fire, which started at 10.50 o'clock yesterday morning, devastated practically the entire central business district of Baltimore and at midnight the flames were still raging with as much fury as at the beginning.

To all appearances Baltimore's business section is doomed. Many of the principal banking institutions, all the leading trust companies, all the largest wholesale houses, all the newspaper offices, many of the principal retail stores and thousands of smaller establishments went up in flame, and in most cases the contents were completely destroyed.

What the loss will be in dollars no man can even estimate, but the sum will be so gigantic that it is hard for the average

of firemen when a live trolley wire fell on him at the corner of Liberty and Baltimore streets, knocking him senseless, and he had to be carried to his home and placed in bed. By this accident the city was deprived of the services of its most experienced and trusted firefighter, and, although District Chief Emerich, who succeeded Chief Horton in command on the ground, did apparently all that was possible, those present could not but regret that Chief Horton was not there.

Mayor McLane came down and was on the ground until a late hour in the night. He walked around the burning district and conferred with various officials as to the steps necessary to be taken at various stages of the fire.

It is thought the loss will be over $50

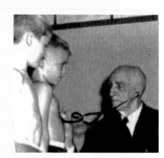

∞ Professors began depositing lecture fees in a central fund and earned salaries rather than selling tickets directly to students (as had been the case since 1807). This was an attempt to mitigate the ongoing financial difficulties created by the proprietary system.

∞ **Archibald "Moonlight" Graham**, class of 1905, was an outstanding minor league baseball player with the New York Giants. Graham was called up to the major leagues at the end of the 1905 season and played just one inning without recording an at-bat. He abandoned his dream of playing in the major leagues, settling in Chisholm, Minnesota, where he practiced family medicine. His story was re-told in the 1988 movie *Field of Dreams*. Graham's character was played by actor Burt Lancaster.

SUN EXTRA

...NING, FEBRUARY 8, 1904.   PRICE ONE CENT

S BURNED

BALTIMORE

...LDINGS IN RUINS

...TED AT

...) TO $80,000,000

...SOUTHWARD AT 3.30 A. M.

...he Fire Sweeps South
...North To Lexington,
...Houses, Banks,
..., B. And O. Cen=
...ge Buildings.

on both sides byjufire and directed the streams at the buildings from which smoke and flame were pouring, at a distance of only two or three yards.

ACROSS CHARLES STREET.

It was utterly, heartbreakingly useless. The flames darted rapidly from place to place, and soon the entire south side of Fayette street was in the grasp of the flames. Down Fayette to Charles they swept, and in a space of time that seemed incredibly short the building occupied by J. W. Putts & Co. was evidently doomed.

Seeing that nothing could save it Mr. Fendall, acting under instructions from Chief Emerich, decided to destroy the building with dynamite, in the hope of preventing the fire from crossing Charles street. The explosion was successful in accomplishing the object, and the entire corner collapsed instantly, but this had, apparently, no effect upon the progress of the sire, for almost before the sound of the falling walls had died away the building on the east side of Charles street began to blaze, and it was evident that the block between Charles and St. Paul streets was doomed.

CALVERT AND EQUITABLE GO.

In a desperate, but futile, effort to prevent the fire going further to the east, building after building was dynamited in this block, but it was all of no avail. The fire proceeded steadily onward. The Daily Record Building was soon in flames, and not many minutes later the fire had leaped over St. Paul street and the lofty, massive Calvert Building began to emit smoke and flame. The Equitable Building, just over a narrow alley, quickly followed, and these two immense buildings gave forth a glare that lighted the city for miles around.

It was thought that the fire could be prevented from crossing to the north side of Fayette street and here again a desperate stand was made by the firemen. Again it was useless and soon the large building of Hall, Headington & Co., on the ... west corner of Charles and F... streets, was blazing brightly. With s... ly a pause the fire darted across the ... side of Charles street and began to la... the handsome building of the U... Trust Company, while at the same ... the large buildings of the west of ... Headington & Co., occupied by W... Brothers and Oppenheim, Oberndorf ... Co., were aflame throughout.

MILLIONS IN A FEW BLOCKS

A detailed Estimate of Loss In The ... Wholesale District.

A careful and conservative estimate ... the loss in the wholesale business distri... in which the fire originated, places it ... something over $16,007,000. This dist... is bounded by Baltimore, Liberty, Ch... and Lombard streets and contained m... of the largest dry goods, clothing and s... houses in the city, besides two promi... banks—the National Exchange and th... kins Place Savings Bank. The estim... was made for The Sun last nigt by M... George E. Taylor, of the insurance firm ... Jenniss & Taylor, Holliday and W... streets. Mr. Taylor sat in his office dic... ing to a reporter of The Sun until it ... stated that the fire was only a few do... away, when he found it necessary to ... move the valuables and papers from h... office.

HOPKINS PLACE

21—S. Lowman & Co., clothing, $125,000.
23—John E. Hurst & Co., storage, $150,000.
25—Findlay, Roberts & Co., hardware, $75,000.
27—Lawrence & Gould Shoe Company and Bates Hat Company, $125,000.
29—S. Ginsberg & Co., clothing, $125,000.
31—Winkelmann & Brown Drug Co., $125,000.
33 and 35—R. M. Sutton & Co. dry goods, $1,500,000.
37—Chesapeake Shoe Company, $100,000.
39—S. F. and A. F. Miller, clothing manufacturers $150,000.
41—S. Halle Sons, boots and shoes, $100,000.
43 and 45—Strauss Bros., dry goods, $250,000.
Rear of 37 and 89—A. C. Meyer & Co. patent medicines, $150,000.

WEST LOMBARD STREET

108 and 110—Matthews Bros., paper-box manufacturers, $75,000.
112 and 114—Strauss, Eiseman & Co., shirt manufacturers, $150,000.
116 and 118—North Bros. & Strauss, have been moving to new building formerly occupied by Heywood Bros.-Wakefield Company, northeast corner Pratt and Greene streets; building $75,000, stock may be about $75,000.

WEST GERMAN STREET

103—Standard Suspender Company and Daniel A. Boone & Co., liquors, $60,000.
105—Bradley, Kirkman, Reese Company, $75,000.
107—George A. Eitel, neckwear manufacturer; Charles L. Linville and J. J. Murphy, sewing silks, $75,000.
109—MCDonald & Fisher, wholesale paper, $100,000.
111—Wiley, Bruster & Co., dry goods, and F. W. & E. Dammann, cloth, $125,000.
113—Henry Oppenheimer & OO., CLOTH*
ING, AND Vansant, Jacobs & Co., shirts, $175,000.
15—Joseph R. Stonebraker & Co., liquors, $75,000.
18—Lewis Lauer & Co., shirts, $100,000.
20—Champion Shoe Manufacturing Company and Diggs, Currin & Co., shirts...

...gh, large modern ... of brick and steel, ...lt of the flimsiest

...f the fire is not, ...ion which started ...es to other build- ...caused by a gaso- ...at Building. Mr. S. ...te street who was ...of Sharp and Bal- ...e fire first broke ...an 10 minutes the ...was a roaring mass ...bottom. When the ...Ball was cut on ...was cut through his ...of glass. ...STREET

and Mr. Roy C. Lafferts, the Government expert, who had comes from Washington especially to take charge of the work of dynamiting the buildings, was on the ground with his apparatus in readiness.

By this time it was thoroughly realized that the flames were completely beyond control and only desperate measures could be expected to relieve the situation. In this strait of City Engineer Fendall and Mr.Lafferty laid a charge in the building adjoining Armstrong, Cator & Co.'s on the west and set it off. The building fell with a crash, but the blazing ruins ignited the Armstrong building and the situation was, if anything, made worse.

Armstrong, Cator & Co.'s building burned rapidly. A large charge of dynamite was let off in it, but the structure

---

1906

ℜ **Samuel T. Darling**, class of 1903, an instructor in histology and pathology, wrote the first clinical and pathological description of a disease associated with tubercle-like lesions in the lungs, liver, spleen and lymph nodes. The disease, known for many years as *Darling's Disease*, was disseminated histoplasmosis. Darling became a world authority as an epidemiologist and tropical disease expert, and he was nominated for the Nobel Prize. In 1923, he applied the "spleen index" rather than the medical history and blood smear as an indicator of the extent and severity of malaria in the U.S. His work included the more accurate technique of examining children and adults while they reclined. He earned international recognition for his laboratory research and field epidemiologic studies of malaria, hookworm disease and dysenteric disorders, particularly amoebic dysentery.

Darling became a world authority as an epidemiologist and tropical disease expert, and he was nominated for the Nobel Prize.

1807   1907

The Regents of the University of Maryland

request the honor of your presence
at the

Centennial Celebration
of the

University of Maryland

Thursday, May 30th to Sunday, June 2nd inclusive

nineteen hundred and seven

according to the accompanying program

Baltimore, Maryland

R. S. U. P.

1907~1919

1907

University of Maryland
e honor of your presence
at the
Centennial Celebration
of the
University of Maryland
Thursday, May 30th to Sunday, June 2nd inclusive
nineteen hundred and seven
according to the accompanying program
Baltimore, Maryland

Dr. John C. Hemmeter, chairman of the centennial committee, at the opening ceremony in Anatomical Hall

fter a taxing first century, many celebrated the school's centennial with great optimism.

Completion of a four-year high school program was now a requirement for admission, with written examinations and uniform grading firmly established. Tuition and fees for a four-year medical education cost $570, with a discount for advance payment. Enrollment stood at 350. Sixty-four instructors constituted the medical faculty, teaching in laboratories of anatomy, chemistry, normal histology and embryology, and pathological histology and bacteriology.

1907

There was also a clinical laboratory. Clinical instruction was administered in a number of locations including University Hospital's lying-in and out-patient departments, the Presbyterian Eye, Ear and Throat Charity Hospital, the Hospital for the Relief of Crippled and Deformed Children, and Bayview Hospital. In addition to University Hospital, there were three buildings dedicated to medical education as well as a library with 7,000 volumes. Since 1902, the medical school term had been expanded from five and a half to seven months.

Since being re-chartered as the University of Maryland in 1812, the institution had added departments of law, dentistry, pharmacy, and a training school for nurses at the hospital. In addition, a letters & sciences department was added in January through an affiliation agreement with St. John's College in Annapolis. After initially ruling that the centennial would center on only the medical department, the regents reversed themselves and announced that a celebration of the whole university was more appropriate. They were hoping the event could elevate the institution to true university status.

The centennial celebration was scheduled for May 30 through June 2. More than 8,000 engraved invitations were mailed to alumni, friends, and presidents of every institution of higher learning in America, as well as most foreign universities. Each building on campus was shrouded in green oak leaves and bunting featuring the university's colors of maroon and black, the state's black and gold, and the country's red, white, and blue. The celebration was centered around the university's annual commencement.

Ceremonies began on Thursday, May 30, in Anatomical Hall of the medical building with the playing of Beethoven's Leonore Overture No. 2 and a welcome to more than 50 delegates representing universities and colleges. Among them were dignitaries from Harvard, Princeton, Cambridge, and the University of Berlin. Thursday events included a luncheon, campus tours, reunions, class dinners and smokers. The highlights of the celebration—graduation ceremonies and a banquet— were held at the Lyric on Friday for 4,000 supporters. The four-hour commencement ceremony included the awarding of 237 degrees from the various departments, plus 30 honorary degrees. Attendees included U.S. attorney general Charles J. Bonaparte, Maryland governor Edwin Warfield, Baltimore mayor J. Barry Mahool and Baltimore archbishop James Gibbons. Saturday featured a steamboat ride from Baltimore to St. John's College in Annapolis for a concert, reception and presentation of a plaque commemorating the affiliation agreement. Ceremonies concluded on Sunday with a service at Mount Vernon Church.

The *Baltimore American* newspaper referred to the event as "the greatest gathering of scholars and educators that Baltimore has ever witnessed." By all accounts the celebration was a smashing success, but it would become evident over the next few years that the celebration neither improved the institution's financial predicament, nor changed public perception that Maryland was nothing more than a string of professional schools.

1909

1908

› **Nathaniel G. Keirle**, class of 1858, published the first monograph on rabies in Maryland stemming from his experimental studies and personal observations. He practiced medicine in Baltimore and served as the city's medical examiner.

› **William H. Arthur**, class of 1877, was named the first commanding officer of Walter Reed Army Hospital in Washington, D.C. A brigadier general in the U.S. Army, Arthur was a distinguished surgeon who also served as commandant of the Army Medical School until retirement in 1918.

› The medical school's library relocated to an old church building on the southeast corner of Lombard and Greene Streets. The building was given the name *Davidge Hall* in honor of the medical school's founder and first dean, Dr. John B. Davidge.

› The first mention of autopsies being performed, with permission of City Hall, was made in a school circular. Third-year students were said to have the advantage of following the case "from the ward to the autopsy room."

By the turn of the century, dissecting cadavers was acceptable to the general public.

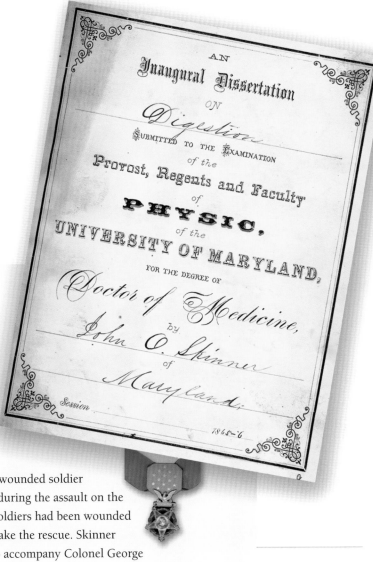

Richardson became physician to U.S. president William H. Taft.

1910

⁏ **James J. Richardson**, class of 1889, became personal physician to U.S. president William H. Taft. Recognized as one of the leading nose and throat specialists in the country, Richardson served in the same capacity for presidents Theodore Roosevelt and Warren G. Harding.

1913

⁏ **Reid Hunt**, class of 1896, was named the first chief of the division of pharmacology at Harvard Medical School. His major interest was the significant biological action of acetylcholine on blood pressure. A Johns Hopkins-trained scientist, Hunt in 1902 reported findings on the toxicity of methyl alcohol.

1915

⁏ **John O. Skinner**, class of 1866, was awarded the Congressional Medal of Honor by President Woodrow Wilson for services performed during the Indian Wars. An assistant surgeon in the U.S. Army Medical Corps, Skinner rescued a wounded soldier who lay under heavy fire during the assault on the Modoc stronghold. Two soldiers had been wounded in an earlier attempt to make the rescue. Skinner was one of four officers to accompany Colonel George F. Crook, commander of the Department of Arizona, in the investigation of the Navajo-Apache country. In 1886, Skinner was appointed U.S. Custodian of Geronimo during the Indian leader's imprisonment at Fort Marion in St. Augustine, Florida.

Skinner with Geronimo

⁏ **Arthur M. Shipley**, class of 1902, was named acting dean.

An Abbreviated Time Line of the Medical School's Growth and Development

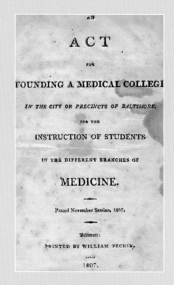

The College of Medicine of Maryland was founded.

1877

Washington University School of Medicine merged with The College of Physicians and Surgeons, bringing City Hospital under control of The College of Physicians and Surgeons.

1807

1827

1876

1872

1812

The College of Medicine of Maryland was re-chartered as the University of Maryland.

The Washington Medical College opened in Baltimore. It was Maryland's first rival medical school in the city and later changed its name to the Washington University School of Medicine.

The College of Physicians and Surgeons of Baltimore City was established.

Maryland Women's Hospital was founded. It was Maryland's first hospital for diseases of women.

Maryland Women's Hospital became affiliated with The College of Physicians and Surgeons.

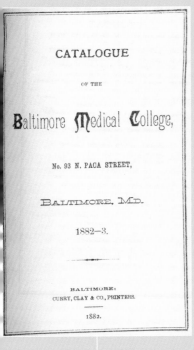

CATALOGUE

OF THE

Baltimore Medical College,

No. 93 N. PACA STREET,

BALTIMORE, MD.

1882—3.

BALTIMORE:
CURRY, CLAY & CO., PRINTERS.

1882.

The Baltimore
Medical College
was founded.

City Hospital became
Mercy Hospital and
remained under control
of The College of
Physicians and
Surgeons.

The Flexner Report
was released. It led
to consolidation and
elimination of many
of the nation's
medical colleges.

The College of Physicians and
Surgeons merged with Maryland.

1881

1909

1910

1913

1915

1920

1884

Maryland and the
College of Physicians
and Surgeons
assumed joint control
over resident medical
appointments at Bay
View Hospital.

The Baltimore Medical College merged with
Maryland. The acquired medical building became
the home of Maryland General Hospital and was
used for teaching by Maryland faculty.

The University of Maryland
merged with the Maryland
State College of Agriculture
in College Park, creating
The University of Maryland,
Baltimore and
College Park.

BULLETIN
OF THE
UNIVERSITY OF MARYLAND SCHOOL OF MEDICINE
AND
COLLEGE OF PHYSICIANS AND SURGEONS

Successor to THE HOSPITAL BULLETIN, of the University of Maryland, BALTIMORE MEDICAL COLLEGE NEWS, and the JOURNAL of the Alumni Association of the College of Physicians and Surgeons

VOL. I   JUNE, 1916   No. 1

MANY have labored earnestly for the interests of the University of Maryland, but none has wrought more mightily than Randolph Winslow. Its interests have been his interest. His has been a labor of love. Unselfishly he has given without stint, time and money, thereby hoping to realize a larger and broader University. Graduating with the class of 1873, practically ever since he has in some capacity or other been associated with the teaching force, the last twenty-five years of which have been spent as a member of the Major Faculty and Board of Regents. At all times a progressive, with the advance of years he has not been a laggard but wide-awake to the possibilities attendant the adoption of modern ideas in medical education. It was mainly through his efforts that the new University Hospital was built, that the curriculum was advanced from two to three, then later to four years, and the adoption of the premedical requirements, and the consummation of the various mergers. Though past 60, he is fortunately in full possession of a virile body and mind, and still takes an active interest in creating and determining the policies of the institution. For more than forty years during stress and strain he has ever turned his face toward the morning, never the setting sun. His has been a work well done, it is our ... half decades. In recognition of a work well done, it is our ... to inscribe this, the initial number of the ...slow, A.M., M.D., LL.D., Professor of Surgery ... and, a skillful and dexterous operator, a gifted ... fight unswervingly for what he considers right, ... hy of the honor.

1916

    Volume I of the *Bulletin* of the University of Maryland School of Medicine was published. It combined former publications of the three recently merged medical schools—Maryland, Baltimore Medical College, and College of Physicians and Surgeons. It became America's oldest medical alumni publication.

    James M. H. Rowland, class of 1892, was named dean.

Dr. James M. H. Rowland
(Dean 1916–40)

James M. H. Rowland was born in Cecil County, Maryland. After attending the West Nottingham Academy, Rowland taught school for two years on Maryland's Eastern Shore to earn money to study medicine. He graduated from Maryland in 1892. Rowland was appointed professor of obstetrics in 1915.

More than anyone in Baltimore, Rowland was conscious of the indifference with which society and the medical profession treated obstetrical patients. When he graduated from medical school and developed an interest in obstetrics, he found that most poor, inner-city mothers were under the care of midwives. Rowland looked askance at this and was instrumental in creating laws to govern the activities of midwives. As a result, both maternal and infant mortality decreased.

Through Rowland's efforts, a hospital program for obstetrical patients was developed along with an outpatient clinic that supervised at-home deliveries. In spite of opposition, Rowland advocated for the practice of episiotomy and for Caesarian section in patients with placenta praevia.

A modest and humble man, Rowland recalled that he had been appointed dean of the medical school "when I had no flair for it." Nevertheless, an editorial in the December 20, 1936, edition of the Baltimore *Sun* praised Rowland for "the fine work that has been done in building the medical school of the University of Maryland to its present high rank." The *Sun* described Rowland as "a citizen who has answered many calls to public service, as a physician whose career is one of hard work and untiring effort to relieve suffering, and as a teacher who makes an indelible impression upon medical students." Rowland died in 1954.

Nathan Winslow, class of 1901

1917

ଛ୦ University of Maryland Base Hospital Number 42 was created and served with distinction in France during World War I. Physicians, surgeons, nurses and assistants from Maryland staffed the unit. It remained active until 1919.

Letter to the *Bulletin* editor:

As I have been fortunate enough to find a piece of paper and a very bad pen, I shall write you. I left America not knowing a soul, but came across with the Roosevelt Hospital unit from New York. I expect you know Drs. Peck, Russel and Floyd. They are all Majors in the unit. We were separated at Liverpool so I don't know where they are. While in London I saw Jenkins. He is at a hospital near London doing ear and throat work with a Dr. O'Malley. He told me that Toulson was in the North of England somewhere, but that Callahan had been sent on to France. I had six days in England and then was sent out here. Am with a field ambulance belonging to a Scotch division.

To give one an idea of your impressions here is a man's sized job, for it is entirely unlike anything I have ever dreamed. First you are struck by the most appalling noise. Everywhere it is whiz bang, crash, boom, etc. The nights have a luridness that makes Dante's picture of hell fade into utter insignificance. You hear the whistle of a shell, then the explosion, followed by falling buildings. You soon learn, unconsciously, to judge a shell by its sound, whether it will come near or far, though if near you are helpless to protect yourself. Apropos of that, it is remarkable what moral courage a roof over your head gives, whether it be of canvass or the roof of a building, though both give no protection at all. At all times, day and night, men are marching past in smaller or larger bodies. As to work, you are overwhelmed at times and do nothing at others, the latter very rare, however. Men are brought in batches of 20 to 50 with every conceivable kind of wounds. Head, chest, abdominal, fractures, etc., etc. throughout the whole category. The worst are sent on back to casualty dressing stations after arresting hemorrhage and applying dressings. At present I am in charge of what is called a Divisional Rest Station. We are in an old Nunnery and have about 350 patients, I being the only medical man (doctor) here. You work and work till you are ready to drop and then work some more. I haven't taken off my clothes in over two days. Was relieved today for twelve hours so am writing in peace. To me the most alarming cases were those who had been gassed. I would like to tell you all about them that I have noticed but this is the only piece of paper I have, and it is a long story. The field ambulance has seven doctors, one lieutenant colonel who is administrator only. All are excellent fellows, quite a lot older than I am, the average age being about forty I guess.

If I come out of this O.K., I shall certainly have seen such things that you could see nowhere else but here. Hear I am to be transferred to our troops as soon as a sufficient number come across.

You will pardon use of both sides of paper and scribble for we have to write under adverse circumstances, to put it mildly.

Hoping that you are enjoying the best of health, I am,

> *Yours sincerely,*
> *John E. Evans, U of M 1916*
> *1st Lieutenant with the 45th field Ambulance, B. E. F. France*

1918

*I*t was announced that beginning with the session 1918–19, women students would be admitted to the medical school on equal terms with men. This innovation had been advocated for some time, but it was only on January 8 that the faculty passed the resolution to admit them. There were several reasons necessitating this: first, there was a shortage of physicians due to the war; second, the medical school was receiving an appropriation from the state, and it was not right that one-half of the youth of the state would be excluded from the benefit of this appropriation; and third, women had for years been admitted to the schools of dentistry and pharmacy, and they had made excellent students.

Herbert H. Haynes, class of 1908, developed the skeletal fixation splint, later know as the *Haynes splint*. A general surgeon, Haynes gained recognition as a surgical inventor of national repute. He introduced new operations and operative techniques, particularly in the field of abdominal surgery, and many were published in the scientific literature. He was also the inventor of a new type of hospital bed.

1917

Burt J. Asper, class of 1911, was ship's surgeon aboard the U.S.S. Cyclops when it mysteriously vanished in the Bermuda Triangle. The auxiliary ship was responsible for delivering coal to Navy warships. After departing Rio de Janeiro, the ship headed northward for Baltimore, issuing its last communication from Barbados. The Navy never offered an explanation for its disappearance, and the ship was never found.

The influenza pandemic known as the Spanish Flu forced school administrators to suspend fall classes. There was considerable sickness among the students, according to the October *Bulletin*, but "fortunately with but slight mortality." The illness afflicted young adults, and pneumonia was identified as the most serious complication. The virus was thought to have originated in Spain and spread rapidly from the transport of troops fighting in the war. In Baltimore, hospitals were deemed "off-limits" to visitors as most of the nurses and resident staffs had been ravaged by the illness. Health authorities took drastic measures to limit the spread of the disease, closing all schools and colleges, movie theatres, concert halls, and churches. It is estimated that the virus killed between 20 and 40 million people throughout the world including 600,000 Americans.

1919

so **Louis H. Douglass**, class of 1911, stressed the importance of prenatal care and was recognized as a leader and innovator in the campaign to continue to lower maternal and infant mortality. Through his efforts, pre-natal clinics were established in Baltimore. He worked with the commissioner of health in founding the Maryland Bureau of Maternal and Child Hygiene and was co-founder of the maternal mortality conferences. At Maryland, Douglass served as professor and head of obstetrics from 1937 to 1955. He was one of the organizers of the Baltimore Rh-Blood Typing Laboratory, a unique development sponsored by the Maryland State Obstetrical and Gynecological Society, and he served as its first president. This represented a significant advance in infant health. An additional contribution made by Douglass was his comprehensive management of patients with eclampsia.

so **John Sliupas**, class of 1891, was appointed Lithuanian ambassador to Latvia and Estonia. A native Lithuanian, he spoke five languages by the time he graduated from high school in Latvia and began his studies at the University of Moscow. Protesting in support of a free Lithuanian press, he became engaged in anti-Czarist activities. Fleeing to New York City in 1884, Sliupas worked to preserve the heritage and language of Lithuanians living in America. He practiced medicine in America until 1917. He helped organize the Lithuanian diplomatic mission in London and served as the Lithuanian delegate at the Paris Peace Conference prior to his ambassadorship. When Sliupas died at age 83, he had authored more than 70 books.

so **Louis A. Buie**, class of 1915, was named chief of the department of proctology at the Mayo Clinic. He was appointed professor of surgery there in 1935, where he invented numerous instruments and authored a widely-used textbook on proctology. His inventions included the Buie Proctologic Table, the development of intra-rectal photographic techniques, the electro-surgical treatment of polyps of the rectum, the Buie Clamp and the Buie Proctoscope. He was responsible for the first complete revision of *Principles of Medical Ethics of the American Medical Association*.

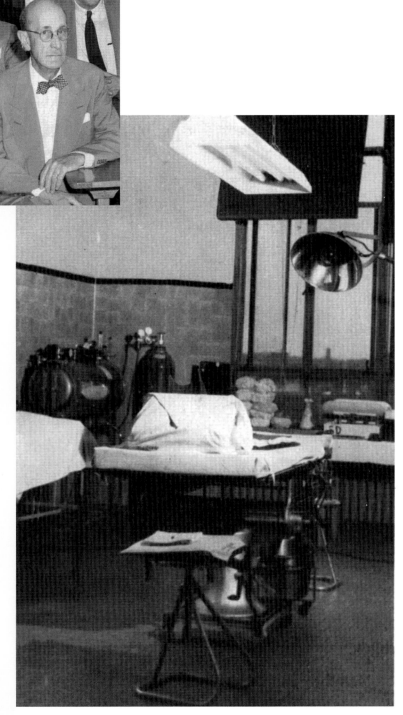

A delivery room during the Douglass era

The Alumni Association of the School of Medicine of the University of Maryland, Incorporated.

SIX PER CENT. SECURED BOND

NOT NEGOTIABLE

The Alumni Association of the School of Medicine of the University of Maryland, Incorporated, a corporation without capital stock, organized and existing under the laws of the State of Maryland, herein referred to as the corporation, acknowledges itself indebted, and for value received promises to pay to the owner of this certificate who is

.... * * * M A U R I C E C. P I N C O F F S * * * ....
as shown by the books of the corporation, the sum of

.... – – – ONE HUNDRED – – – ....dollars on or before the 1st day of January 1940, with interest thereon at the rate of six per cent per annum (6%) accounting from the 1st day of January 1930 and payable by check to the owner hereof as aforesaid in semi-annual installments on the 1st day of July 1930 and thereafter every six months until the principal amount hereof is fully paid.

This bond is payable at the office of the corporation on the day named but it may be retired on any interest date by payment of the principal amount hereof with interest as aforesaid.

This bond is one of a series not exceeding in the aggregate the sum of thirty thousand dollars ($30,000.00) secured by a Deed of Trust of the property situated in Baltimore City, in the State of Maryland, and known as 519 West Lombard Street, executed by the corporation to Richard C. Bernard, Trustee, and recorded among the Land Records of said City in Liber S. C. L. 4980, folio 199, reference to which is made for a particular description of said property and the terms and conditions upon which this bond is issued. The above mentioned property is subject to certain prior mortgages and the corporation agrees that any funds in excess of twelve thousand dollars ($12,000.00) derived from the issue of bonds of this series will be applied to the reduction thereof.

This bond shall be valid only when authenticated by the trustee as one of the bonds secured by the aforementioned Deed.

This bond is not negotiable and may be transferred on the books of the corporation in person or by attorney only upon presentation of this certificate duly endorsed by the owner thereof, in the presence of a witness who shall affix his or her signature, on the reverse hereof.

No personal liability whatever, by virtue of any Statute or otherwise, shall be incurred by any member, director, officer or agent of the corporation, or by the trustee or any successor or successors, by virtue of this obligation or of the said Deed of Trust.

The execution and delivery of this bond, and the payment of interest thereon, has been authorized and directed by resolutions of the members of the corporation and of the board of directors thereof.

IN WITNESS WHEREOF, the said corporation has caused these presents to be signed in its corporate name by its President and its corporate seal affixed, attested by its secretary or assistant secretary, on this 20th day of February , in the year nineteen hundred and thirty.

THE ALUMNI ASSOCIATION OF THE SCHOOL OF MEDICINE OF THE UNIVERSITY OF MARYLAND, INCORPORATED.

By _____
Its President

Its Corporate SEAL.

Attest: _____
Its Assistant Secretary

This is to certify that this bond is one of the bonds secured by the deed of trust within mentioned.

_____
Trustee

Chapter Six

1920~1940

NOTICE TO STUDENTS

The personal expenses of the students are at least as low or more as in any large city in the United States. The follow mates of a student's personal expenses for the academic year months have been prepared by students, and are based up experience. In addition to these the student must bear in expenditure for a microscope.

1920

or 113 years, generations of Maryland's governing regents had labored to advance their *private* institution. At their own expense they constructed medical buildings and a hospital. They repelled a takeover by the state in 1826. On more than one occasion they upgraded admission standards and graduation requirements—bold revisions that improved the quality of their school but also threatened its solvency. And they aggressively acquired, through merger agreements, two competing medical schools in the city.

As they looked to the future, revenues from an increasing enrollment base were critical to funding the university's operations and servicing its debt. Recent enrollment spikes in schools of dentistry, pharmacy and law were keeping the institution afloat, but they were also crowding the campus. Secondary income streams from the state and the institution's endowment were at best meager. On the academic side, the prospects for improvement were not any better. Although Maryland's affiliation agreement with St. John's College now entered its 13th year, the Annapolis-based institution's refusal to agree to a formal merger was preventing Maryland from meeting its educational requirements as a university.

With promises of financial backing from the state, the governing regents were ready for change. During the January 1920 session, the General Assembly of Maryland passed Chapter 480, an act to merge and consolidate Maryland with the State College of Agriculture effective July 1. The regents assented at a meeting on May 20, agreeing to relinquish their control of the school. On July 1, 1920, the University of Maryland, Baltimore and College Park was born. Albert F. Woods, AM, DAgr, was appointed president. He was guided by a board of regents whose members had no connection to the teaching faculties. The long struggle ended with the birth of a *public* university.

At the time, there were 15 hospitals associated with or connected to the University of Maryland School of Medicine:

University Hospital

Mercy Hospital

Maryland General Hospital

Franklin Square Hospital

Maternity Hospital of the University of Maryland

Maryland Lying-in Hospital, adjoining Maryland General Hospital

West End Maternity, adjoining Franklin Square Hospital

Municipal Hospitals—Baltimore City Hospitals (Bay View)

Presbyterian Eye, Ear and Throat Charity Hospital

James Lawrence Kernan Hospital and Industrial School of Maryland for Crippled Children

St. Elizabeth Home of Baltimore City for Colored Children

St. Vincent's Infant Asylum

Sheppard and Enoch Pratt Hospital

Mount Hope Retreat for the Insane

Nursery and Child's Hospital of Baltimore City

In addition, three outpatient dispensaries were functioning for the clinical instruction of medical students. They were located in University Hospital, Mercy Hospital, and Maryland General Hospital.

University of Maryland president Albert F. Woods

1920

୫ **Dr. William H. Schultz** was appointed professor of pharmacology, a position he held until 1931. Schultz was recognized for his work on the mechanism of anaphylactic shock, and the Schultz-Dale reaction was the outgrowth of some of his fundamental studies on anaphylaxis. He was also a pioneer in the early studies on adrenaline.

1921

୫ **Mervin T. Sudler**, class of 1901, was named dean of the Kansas University School of Medicine, a position he held until 1924. Sudler was a fellow of the American College of Surgeons.

୫ **Henry A. Cotton**, class of 1899, lecturing before a packed house at Princeton University, revealed his theory in the understanding and treatment of mental disorder—that madness was caused by focal sepsis. He claimed to cure 85 percent of his psychotic patients after identifying and eliminating infections in the body. This began with removal of the most obvious sources of infection—teeth and tonsils—and if necessary continued with resections of internal organs—colon, spleen, cervix, and stomach. Cotton, superintendent of the New Jersey State Hospital in Trenton, had impeccable credentials. He trained at Johns Hopkins under Dr. Adolf Meyer and performed additional psychiatric research in Germany. He had no formal surgical training and persisted with this treatment for more than 10 years even after mounting evidence indicated that at least one third of his patients died. It was estimated that hundreds had been killed or maimed by Cotton before his death in 1933. Some of his techniques continued to be employed for more than 25 years after his death. Cotton's two sons, who had their teeth extracted as a prophylactic measure, committed suicide as adults.

1922

୫ **John S. Fulton**, class of 1881, was appointed director of the Maryland State Board of Health. Upon receiving his medical degree, Fulton developed an interest in tuberculosis and limited his practice largely to that disease. He was appointed to the faculty at Maryland as professor in 1902. Fulton led the campaign for the enactment of the first registration law that required reports to be made of patients with tuberculosis. In 1904, he planned and supervised the first tuberculosis exposition held in Baltimore and was largely instrumental in the formation of the National Tuberculosis Association.

1923

୫ **Theresa Ora Snaith** became the first woman to graduate from the medical school. Snaith transferred to Maryland from the Women's Medical College in Philadelphia at the end of her second year. Upon graduation she practiced medicine in West Virginia.

୫ **Dr. Gordon Wilson**, professor and chairman of the department of medicine from 1913 to 1922, was elected president of the American Clinical and Climatological Association, one of the country's most prestigious internal medicine organizations. Following his death in 1932, the Gordon Wilson Hall for lectureships was established at the medical school.

Eva F. Dodge became Maryland's first female rotating intern and resident in obstetrics and gynecology.

1927

Arthur M. Shipley, class of 1902 and chairman of the department of surgery, demonstrated the need for performing pericardiotomy for purulent pericarditis. Shipley served in World War I as commanding officer and surgeon of Evacuation Hospital 8 in France, earning several military awards including the Distinguished Service Medal. Upon his return to Maryland, Shipley was appointed to the professorship of surgery. He taught for 46 years at the medical school, holding the chair of surgery for 28 years beginning in 1920. During this time the development of surgical specialties was in its infancy at Maryland when compared to other leading medical schools. Hampered by old and ill-equipped laboratories, an outdated hospital, and minimal support from the state, Shipley pressed forward, establishing sub-departments of neurosurgery, genitourinary surgery, orthopaedics, thoracic & vascular surgery, and plastic surgery.

1925

Eva F. Dodge, class of 1925, became Maryland's first female rotating intern and resident in obstetrics and gynecology. Her career spanned five decades as a physician, educator, consultant and public health administrator covering eight states, South America, Europe and the Orient. In 1945, she joined the University of Arkansas in the department of obstetrics and gynecology. Upon the announcement of her retirement in 1964, Dodge received professor emerita status, the first such appointment at Arkansas. In 1967, she became the first woman to receive Maryland's Honor Award and Gold Key.

John S. B. Woolford, class of 1896, organized the Roswell, New Mexico Automobile Club. Earlier a popular surgeon in Chattanooga, Tennessee, he was forced by ill health into a wheelchair in 1918 and, subsequently, into retirement. Relocating to New Mexico, Woolford was elected to three terms as president of the Roswell Chamber of Commerce. He became president of and helped develop both the Fort Worth-Roswell-Los Angeles and the Carlsbad Cavern-Petrified Forest-Grand Canyon highways.

George E. Bennett, class of 1909, organized America's first rural crippled children's clinic in Lonaconing, Maryland. The project was used as a model for the creation of other such clinics throughout the United States. A senior faculty member at Johns Hopkins, Bennett was elected president of the American Orthopaedic Association and the American Academy of Orthopaedic Surgeons, and he perfected various orthopaedic surgical procedures. In 1923, he began treating major league baseball players for bone, tendon and joint injuries and quickly developed a national reputation.

Players visiting his office included Dizzy Dean, Lefty Gomez, Dixie Walker, Joe DiMaggio, Phil Rizzuto, and Pee Wee Reese. In Dr. Bennett's desk drawer was a photograph of DiMaggio, Tommy Henrich, Charlie Keller and Frankie Crosetti in their Yankee uniforms with an inscription: "To Dr. George, the man who made this picture possible." Bennett was recognized by many as the father of sports medicine.

1927

∾ **Dr. Eduard C. A. Uhlenhuth**,

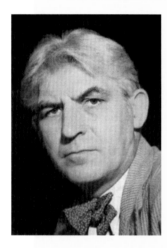

associate professor of anatomy at Maryland, was credited with the discovery that the anterior lobe of the pituitary gland secretes a thyrotropic hormone. The contribution won Uhlenhuth the Van Meter Prize in 1936. Uhlenhuth became chairman of the anatomy department in 1936, a position he held until retirement in 1955. He published more than 200 scientific articles, was author of a widely used monograph *Problems in the Anatomy of the Pelvis* (1953), and a translation of Sobotta's *Atlas of Descriptive Human Anatomy*.

1928

∾ **Theodore M. Davis**, class of 1914, in collaboration with an electrical engineer, invented the electromagnetic switch, permitting the use of the cutting current and coagulating current through one electrode. The invention established Davis as the father of the modern approach to transurethral surgery and prostatic resections. His contributions to urology merited consideration of a Nobel Prize in 1965.

∾ **Oliver S. Lloyd**, class of 1909, was named surgeon for the Baltimore City Fire Department, an appointment he held for 28 years. A capable surgeon, Lloyd invented the Lloyd Lag Screw and Lloyd Hip Screw, ingenious instruments for internal fixation of fractures of the neck and femur. These screws were used successfully for years by general surgeons and orthopaedists.

1935

so **Frank Bressler**, class of 1885, a surgeon at the Hebrew (Sinai) Hospital and local surgeon for the Pennsylvania Railroad Company, died. He left $1.2 million in a bequest to benefit the medical school. Some $280,000 was matched with state funds to construct the Bressler Building for Research at 29 S. Greene Street. The state attempted to move the remainder of the endowment from the Trustees of the Endowment Fund of the University of Maryland, Inc., to a general university fund; but the Maryland Court of Appeals upheld the terms of Bressler's will, and the medical school remained the beneficiary.

so **Dr. Magnus I. Gregersen**, professor of physiology and chairman of the department from 1935 to 1937, affirmed the value and reliability of the Evans blue dye method of determining plasma volume and the application of this method in evaluating changes in plasma in shock and various disease states. His observations were significant and helpful in the understanding of deranged cardiovascular function and served as effective guides to corrective treatment.

so **Jacob H. Conn**, class of 1929, was the first practicing psychiatrist in Maryland to be certified by the American Board of Psychiatry and Neurology. Conn became an internationally renowned expert in the field of hypnosis and authored more than 100 publications in the field of psychotherapy, child psychiatry and hypnosis. He developed the "Play Interview" treatment of fearful children, the method of hypnosynthesis, and he pioneered treatment for sex offenders and sociopaths. An assistant professor emeritus of psychiatry and lecturer in hypnosis at Johns Hopkins, Conn successfully treated Baltimore Oriole Paul Blair, who developed lingering fear in the batter's box after a 1970 pitch hit him in the face, causing serious eye and facial injuries.

The focus of medicine at Maryland shifted from theoretical to practical courses and from education geared toward future private practice to education designed to promote public service. During the New Deal era, salaries of full professors ranged from $3,100 to $7,000 per annum. The idea was to avoid a rigid pay schedule and encourage across-the-board raises in order to attract the most highly qualified teachers.

Conn became an internationally renowned expert in the field of hypnosis and authored more than 100 publications in the field of psychotherapy, child psychiatry and hypnosis.

1936

🔊 Following the stock market crash of 1929, the Medical Alumni Association, overburdened with debt in running the university's bookstore and cafeteria, filed for bankruptcy and eventually discontinued operating both entities. The Association immediately reorganized itself under the direction of **William H. Triplett**, class of 1911, who guided association activities for more than 50 years.

🔊 A new "curative workshop" at University Hospital, operated by the Junior League under supervision of the doctors, was opened to provide occupational therapy for cardiac, orthopaedic and psychiatric patients.

🔊 Indigent patients gained a new location to receive treatment, as the "old" hospital building on the southwest corner of Lombard and Greene streets was converted into a dispensary, the largest such facility south of New York.

1938

🔊 The first case in Maryland of disseminated histoplasmosis was reported by **Dr. Robert B. Wright**, professor of pathology until 1961, and **Dr. Frank W. Hachtel**, chairman of the department of bacteriology from 1924 to 1954. The disease had initially been described by Dr. Samuel Darling during his work in the Panama Canal in 1906. At that time Dr. Darling warned that the disease would one day reach Baltimore.

🔊 **Francis C. Hertzog**, class of 1917, became one of the first medical examiners with the Civil Aeronautics Board. He issued a pilot medical certificate to famed pilot Douglas "Wrong Way" Corrigan prior to his misdirected flight from New York to Dublin.

Dr. Frank W. Hachtel

1939

🔊 **Edward F. Cotter**, class of 1935, reported the first case of Boeck's sarcoid with predominant cardiac involvement. Cotter later headed the teaching division of physical diagnosis in Maryland's department of medicine.

1940

🔊 **Dr. H. Boyd Wylie** was named dean.

Dr. H. Boyd Wylie

(Dean 1940–43, 1946–54)

After serving as both assistant and acting dean in the early 1940s, H. Boyd Wylie was officially named dean at Maryland in June 1948. A native of Baltimore, Wylie graduated from the Johns Hopkins University in 1908 and earned a medical degree there in 1912. He was appointed to the Maryland faculty in 1913, and was later named professor and chair of biochemistry.

Wylie's career at Maryland spanned 41 years. At one point in the 1940s, he simultaneously served as the head of biochemistry, chairman of the admissions committee, and acting dean of the faculty. During Wylie's deanship, the medical school accepted its first African-American students. He was considered tough but fair, and was a father figure to many of his students. Wylie died in 1963 at age 76. ∞

1940

∞ Five years in the making, the Frank Bressler Research Building opened on Greene Street.

∞ **Ralph F. Davis**, class of 1945, while a senior at the University of Maryland College Park, composed the *Maryland Fight Song*. Davis was an accomplished musician, playing the piano, trumpet, drums, harmonica and sousaphone. He became chief of radiology at Methodist Hospital in Brooklyn, N.Y.

∞ A community hospital in Addison, Michigan, was dedicated as a monument to **Bowers H. Growt**, class of 1916. Working at Maryland General Hospital as a gynecologist until 1920, Growt moved to Addison to open a medical practice. Located in a small rural community with no hospital nearby, he began building the hospital when it was little more than a two-bed infirmary adjoining his office. With no government aid or significant philanthropy, he was assisted by his farm neighbors and former patients who staged benefit shows, dances, church suppers, and rummage sales to help enhance the building fund. The hospital opened at a cost of $15,000.

IN MEMORY OF

BERNARD J. SABATINO, M.D.

UNIVERSITY OF MARYLAND SCHOOL OF MEDICINE
CLASS OF 1938

FIRST LIEUTENANT MEDICAL CORPS
MARYLAND NATIONAL GUARD

CAPTAIN MEDICAL CORPS
ARMY OF THE UNITED STATES

KILLED IN ACTION ON OMAHA BEACH
JUNE 6, 1944

THIS TABLET IS ERECTED BY
HIS ASSOCIATES IN THE MEDICAL SERVICE
OF THE NINTH INFANTRY DIVISION

Chapter Seven

1941~1959

World War II

America's entry into World War II brought changes to the medical school as many of its faculty and hospital staff were sent abroad. The 42nd Medical Hospital, created during World War I, was reactivated and split into two 500-bed units with the creation of the 142nd Hospital. Both units consisted of medical, dental, pharmacy and nursing personnel, and before the war's end both had grown to 2,000 beds.

To assist the war effort, an accelerated academic program was instituted at Maryland. The school year ran from April to December and included a brief three-week break in August. As a result, in 1943, the school graduated two classes. The first group of 97 students finished in March (1943M), and a second group of 90 finished in December (1943D).

Maryland's 142nd Hospital in the Fiji Islands

The 42nd Hospital was located in Australia, and later in the Philippines. Its members served on the hospital ship *Marigold*, the first American vessel to eventually tie up in Tokyo Harbor to help process allied prisoners of war. After a few stops, the 142nd became the largest hospital in the China-Burma-India Theatre.

Maryland graduates served with distinction. In 1942, **Fred W. Rankin**, class of 1909, was appointed chief surgical consultant to the Surgeon General. Rankin had earned a national and international reputation for contributions related to diseases of the colon, and several instruments useful for colonic surgery bore his name. He was a senior surgical staff member at the Mayo Clinic for six years before being appointed chair of surgery at the University of Kentucky in Louisville.

Norman T. Kirk, class of 1910, was appointed Surgeon General of the U.S. Army in 1943, a position he held until retirement in 1947. His medical responsibilities covered oversight of 47,000 doctors, 15,000 dentists and 57,000 nurses caring for 15 million patients. Under his guidance as Surgeon General, the U.S.

1941

99

Army in World War II achieved a record based on recovery from wounds and freedom from complicated disease never before accomplished in wartime history.

Several graduates were recognized for scientific advances. **Theodore E. Woodward**, class of 1938, working at the Pasteur Institute in North Africa as a member of the U.S. Typhus Fever Commission, conducted studies with French authorities which in 1942 showed that one dose of an inactivated typhus

Dr. Theodore E. Woodward

vaccine stimulated antibody formation and was protective against the disease. Additional research soon followed. As an associate professor at Maryland in 1948, Woodward directed initial clinical studies—in collaboration with the Army Medical Service Graduate School—on the efficacy of Chloromycetin. The studies were performed at the Institute of Medical Research in Kuala Lumpur, Malaysia. This medical science team reported the first striking cure for scrub typhus fever with Chloromycetin, earning them a nomination for the Nobel Prize. Later that year additional research led to the dramatic efficacy of Chloromycetin in patients with Rocky Mountain Spotted Fever in Maryland. Woodward served as chairman of the department of medicine at Maryland from 1954 to 1981. In 1942, **Mason Trupp**, class of 1937, invented the first "anti-gravity suit" worn by pilots to prevent them from "blacking out" while quickly ascending after a dive.

Dr. Mason Trupp

Hundreds of alumni were cited for bravery. Captain **Manuel Brown**, class of 1938, was awarded the Silver Star for entering an unmarked mine field to supervise the evacuation of the wounded. Captain **Michael L. DeVincentis**, class of 1941, received the Bronze Star for meritorious achievement as a battalion surgeon, working tirelessly to care for the sick and wounded under extremely adverse weather conditions in the Philippine Islands. Brigadier General **George Rice**, class of 1916, was awarded the Air Medal for participation in hazardous aerial flights in connection with his duties as chief surgeon at the Eighth Army Air Force Headquarters.

Dr. Joshua W. Baxley III

Too many paid the supreme sacrifice. Among those who lost their lives while serving their country were **Thomas J. Coonan**, class of 1925, a major with Maryland's 42nd Hospital in Australia, who died of a severe head injury on November 3, 1942. **Joshua W. Baxley III**, class of 1941, a lieutenant in the Medical Corps of the National Guard, was lost in action as a result of the sinking of the *Bristol* in the Mediterranean on October 13, 1943. And **Bernard J. Sabatino**, class of 1938, a first lieutenant in the Medical Corps of the Maryland National Guard, lost his life on Omaha Beach on D-Day.

Dr. Robert Urie Patterson

(Dean 1943–46)

Major General Robert Urie Patterson was born in Montreal and received his medical degree from McGill University in 1898. He was named dean of the medical school and superintendent of University Hospital, as the board of regents merged the two positions in order to encourage closer coordination as a combined teaching unit.

As dean during the war years, he found the medical school faculty as well as the educational facilities were terribly depleted, yet Patterson's strong personality contributed to the maintenance of high standards. He was instrumental in the creation of a program which eventually expanded the post-graduate training facilities of the medical school, and he initiated a planning committee responsible for the medical school's post-war transitioning.

Patterson served in the U.S. Army from 1901 until retirement in 1935. He received numerous decorations including the Distinguished Service Medal and two Silver Star citations. During the final four years of his career, he served as Surgeon General. Upon retirement from the military but prior to his appointment at Maryland, Patterson was dean of the University of Oklahoma School of Medicine. ∞

Maryland's University Hospital in 1943

1943

∞ **Dr. Robert U. Patterson** was named dean.

1944

∞ **Alice S. Woolley**, class of 1930, was elected president of the American Women's Medical Association. Woolley was active in promoting women physicians in the Armed Forces, and she addressed the Congress on a bill to do so. During World War I, the Poughkeepsie, New York, native was awarded the Medaille de la Reconnaissance Francaise by the French government for two years of service.

1945

℘ **Stanley E. Bradley**, class of 1938, performed the first catheterization of the renal and hepatic veins in a human and was the first to elucidate the hepatic circulation, detecting abnormalities in function through physiologic studies in normal and disease states. Bradley was professor of medicine at the College of Physicians and Surgeons of Columbia University and served as its department chair from 1959 to 1970.

℘ The Baltimore Rh Blood Typing Laboratories opened under the direction of **Milton S. Sacks**, class of 1934, a member of Maryland's faculty. "Uncle Miltie," as he was affectionately called by his students, was a popular hematology professor. The lab was one of the earliest of its kind in the country. The effort was initiated by the medical school, hospital, and the Maryland Obstetrical and Gynecological Society.

1946

The use of a spinal anesthetic to alleviate the pain of childbirth was introduced in Baltimore by Dr. Frederick C. Dye, professor of anesthesiology at the medical school. Maryland was the only institution in the state and one of the few in the world to employ this method early on as standard procedure for obstetrical cases.

1947

℘ **Albert E. Goldstein**, class of 1912, was credited with perfecting the artificial bladder. An internationally recognized urologist, Goldstein taught anatomy and histology at Maryland from 1913 to 1920, and began teaching genito-urinary pathology in 1921. He served as assistant professor in the department until retirement in 1957. In addition, Goldstein headed the division of urology at Baltimore's Sinai Hospital from the time of its founding in 1920 until 1957.

Albert E. Goldstein was credited with perfecting the artificial bladder.

1948

so **Harry M. Robinson Jr.**, class of 1935, initiated studies on the efficacy of broad spectrum antibiotics in patients with the major venereal diseases. These investigations showed that gonorrhea and early syphilis could be effectively treated by oral administration, giving the clinician alternate drugs when penicillin was ill-advised. Robinson was professor and director of the division of dermatology.

1949

so A $25 million legislative appropriation to improve the state's mental hospitals included $3 million earmarked for the creation of a psychiatry department at Maryland. The appointment of professor and chairman went to **Dr. Jacob E. Finesinger** who began at Maryland in 1950. Finesinger came to Maryland from Harvard Medical School and the staff at Massachusetts General Hospital. He pioneered the inclusion of psychiatric principles in the standard clinical history sought from patients in general medicine and surgery. Finesinger became the first director of the medical school's institute for psychiatry and human behavior which opened a few years later as an addition to University Hospital. He remained on the faculty until his death in 1959.

so **Paul E. Carliner**, class of 1934, in association with Dr. Leslie Gay (both on the staff of Johns Hopkins), developed the drug Dramamine to combat seasickness. The two had been testing the drug

as an experimental antihistamine when a female patient suffering from hives reported that her motion sickness on a streetcar was suppressed by taking a dose of the drug in advance of her ride. The two decided to test the drug on soldiers traveling to Germany on the ship *General C.C. Ballou*. The drug became a standard treatment for motion sickness.

Following the end of World War II, the medical school began staffing its clinical departments with full-time salaried physicians, upgraded from part-time.

1950

so **Abraham M. Lilienfeld**, class of 1944, recognized internationally as the foremost figure in the epidemiology of chronic disease, tracked down clues to an amazing variety of chronic
disorders: cerebral palsy, epilepsy, mental retardation, cirrhosis of the liver, gout, hyaline membrane disease, Downs Syndrome, ulcerative colitis, heart disease and stroke. He was especially
noted for work on neoplastic diseases. Lilienfeld was professor of epidemiology at the Johns
Hopkins School of Hygiene and Public Health.

so **Morton I. Levin**, class of 1930, directed the initial convincing study linking cigarette
smoking to the development of lung cancer. His study, published in the *Journal of the American Medical Association*, included an examination
of all patients admitted to Roswell Park Memorial
Hospital in Buffalo, New York, from 1938 to 1950
where Levin was chief of the department of epidemiology. At the time he was also assistant commissioner for medical services for the New York
State Department of Health. Levin developed a
formula for measuring the proportion of all cases
of disease which may be attributable to a risk
factor—known as Levin's Measure of Attributable
Risk. During his career he was a consultant to the
U.S. President's Commission on Heart Disease,
Cancer and Stroke and was a consultant to the National Institutes of Health and
National Cancer Institute. Levin was the author of nearly 100 books and articles con-
cerning lung cancer screening, breast cancer, and other malignant tumors. From 1967
until his death in 1995, he was a visiting professor of epidemiology at Johns Hopkins.

so **John Z. Bowers**, class of 1938, was appointed
dean of the University of Utah School of Medicine, a
position he held until 1955. From 1955 to 1961, he
served in this same capacity at the University of
Wisconsin. His career included a position as deputy
director, division of biology and medicine, at the
U.S. Atomic Energy Commission; president of the
Josiah Macy, Jr. Foundation; and president of Alpha
Omega Alpha. He served as a member of the health
resources advisory committee to Presidents Eisenhower and Kennedy, and published several author-
itative books on Oriental medicine.

so Members in the department of medicine reported the efficacy of corticosteroids
in patients seriously ill with typhoid fever or Rocky Mountain Spotted Fever. Dramatic reductions in toxic signs of
illness and rapid defervescence occurred usually within 24 hours of initiating steroid treatment in conjunction with
antibiotics. The investigators concluded that corticosteroids were therapeutically indicated only in those patients
seriously ill with these diseases who were encountered late in illness, and that broad spectrum antibiotics remained
the mainstay of management.

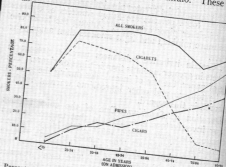

SMOKING—LEVIN ET AL.

J. A. M. A.
May 27, 1950

CANCER AND TOBACCO SMOKING
A Preliminary Report

MORTON L. LEVIN, M.D.
HYMAN GOLDSTEIN, M.D.
and
PAUL R. GERHARDT, M.D.
Albany, N. Y.

The published literature on use of tobacco and its
possible association with human cancer fails to show
clearcut consistent observations. Reviews of the literature for the past twenty years reveals that it is often
conflicting and that it consists for the most part of
studies which are inconclusive because of lack of adequate samples, lack of random selection, lack of proper
controls or failure to age-standardize the data. Potter
and Tully [1] have reported a higher proportion of
smokers in patients with cancer of the "buccal cavity"
and "respiratory tract" among males "over the age of
40" who were seen at Massachusetts cancer clinics.
Since 1938 a history of tobacco usage has been
obtained routinely from all patients admitted to the
Roswell Park Memorial Institute, Buffalo. These his-

Percentage of patients who had ever smoked by type of smoking.

tories are part of the regular clinical history and are
taken before the final diagnosis has been established.
This procedure is considered especially important from
the standpoint of excluding bias. Approximately half
the patients admitted to the institute are subsequently
found not to have cancer. Special attention with respect
to the history of smoking has not been paid to any single
group of conditions, so that these records may be presumed to be free from bias which might result from
preconceived ideas as to relation between smoking and
a particular form of cancer.

The histories record the date smoking began, dura-
tion, type of smoking and amount per day. The reliability of the quantitative aspects of smoking obtained
by a history is of course highly variable. It is presumed,
however, that such errors are not selective with respect
to presence or absence of cancer, especially since only
patients suspected by their physicians of having cancer
are admitted to the Institute.

1951

🔖 **Roderick E. Charles** and **Donald W. Stewart** became Maryland's first African-American students. Graduating in 1955, Charles went on to practice psychiatry on the faculty of SUNY Buffalo. He helped found, staff, and oversee a free medical clinic south of the city for migrant farm workers. Stewart practiced internal medicine in Baltimore for more than fifty years.

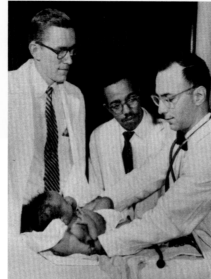

Dr. Roderick E. Charles

Dr. Donald W. Stewart

A new type of pull-out wire for tendon surgery was reported by faculty members Arlie Mansberger, class of 1947; Erwin R. Jennings, class of 1946; Edward P. Smith Jr., class of 1946; and George H. Yeager, class of 1929. The suture consisted of a braided tantalum wire with a welded curved cutting needle at the proximal end, and a welded straight cutting needle at the distal end. It perfected the preexisting device made of twisted stainless steel which proved to be unsatisfactory because it lacked pliability. The tantalum wire suture was extremely flexible, had excellent tensile strength, and was easily removed.

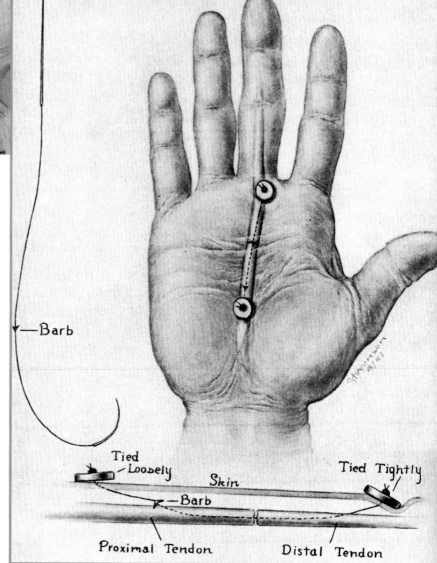

1957

The medical school staged a sesquicentennial celebration concurrently with commencement exercises on June 5 & 6. The Medical Alumni Association had a special coin minted to commemorate the occasion.

Thomas B. Turner, class of 1925, was named dean at Johns Hopkins Medical School, a position he held until 1968. Turner was a nationally recognized authority on infectious diseases.

The University of Maryland Board of Regents approved the transfer of the name Davidge Hall from the medical library to the original medical building in honor of Dr. John B. Davidge, Maryland's founder and first dean.

UNIVERSITY OF MARYLAND
COLLEGE PARK

OFFICE OF THE PRESIDENT

April 22 1958

Dr. William S. Stone, Dean
School of Medicine
University of Maryland
Baltimore 1, Maryland

Dear Dean Stone:

This is to advise you that at a meeting of the Board of Regents on April 16, 1958, the Board passed a motion, unanimously and enthusiastically, that the old Medical School Building constructed in 1812 be named Davidge Hall in honor of Dr. John Davidge. This was done in grateful recognition of the distinguished leadership of Dr. Davidge in the planning of the School of Medicine Building and in establishing the School of Medicine.

The Director of the Physical Plant, Mr. George O. Weber, will assume the responsibility of placing the name on this building.

Sincerely yours,

Wilson H. Elkins
President

WHE/ew

cc: Dr. A. O.

1958

F. Mason Sones Jr., class of 1943D, discovered that the arteries of the human heart could be invaded safely with catheter and dyes in order to photograph their configuration. His technique, cine coronary angiography, became the gold standard for pinpointing coronary artery disease and the basis for selection of surgical candidates and evaluation of other forms of treatment. From 1950 until his death in 1985, Sones was affiliated with the Cleveland Clinic Foundation, serving as director of the cardiac laboratory and pediatric cardiology, and director of the department of cardiovascular disease. He founded the Society for Cardiac Angiography and served as its president. Sones was remembered as the father of modern interventional cardiology.

Dr. Richard B. Hornick and his medical school associates provided clarification of the pathogenesis of typhoid fever and demonstrated the proper dosage of typhoid vaccines. The studies settled the controversial issue prevailing since 1898 regarding the efficacy of typhoid vaccine and provided new guidelines for vaccine dosages. The group initiated studies to evaluate the efficacy of vaccines given orally for immunization against typhoid fever, bacillary dysentery, and Asiatic cholera. Hornick became director of Maryland's division of infectious diseases in 1963 and was made full professor in 1971.

Charles E. Shaw, class of 1944 and faculty member beginning in 1950, published the first clinical report establishing the effectiveness of low doses of insulin in treating diabetic keto-acidosis rather than the conventional high doses.

1959

Joseph E. Schenthal, class of 1939, established the Tulane Medical Computer Center, the first of its kind, and from 1960 to 1963 published several articles in the *Journal of the American Medical Association* on the role of computers in medicine. He was a faculty member at Tulane Medical School in the department of medicine and preventive medicine.

Vol. 114—No. 135

WEATHER

Sunny today, high around 50.
Increasing cloudiness tonight.
Chance of rain tomorrow.
Detailed Report on Page 2.

Fire, Blasts B
U. Of M. Medi

Reds Shoot Up
Large S. Viet
Truck Convoy

Saigon, March 25 (P)—Com
munist forces in the northern
of South Vietnam shot
a 123-truck convoy yester

In skirmishes and mortar
tacks, the Reds killed 24
United States marines and
unded 110

The Communists ambushed
South Vietnamese Army
nvoy near Da Nang base mi
Swift Enemy Raid
and 47 others wounded
In the early battle gun came
ing raising casualties tonight
Detailed Report on Page 2

General Was Target

Anti-Mao Blast Kills
At Least 30, Report

Hong Kong, March 25 (P)—Mao in the Chinese Communist
travelers from Canton today Chairman's prolonged struggle
said 70 persons were killed when gain unchallenged control of
crowded this week when a bomb Red China
meant to assassinate a Red The travelers said the bomb
Chinese Army general exploded went off near the general but
at a rally in support of Mao Tse- exploded outward toward the
tung. They said the general sur- crowd instead of inward toward
vived the platform where he was
"There were 30 or more bodies speaking
on the ground alone after the They said wall posters in
explosion and many more were Canton blamed the bombing on
severely wounded" reported one "revisionist maneuvers"—enemies
these men said he went to of Mao and reported the
one side near the blast "bombing plot" ring
Sent By Mao leader had been caught
Some of the casualties were Meningitis Epidemic
said to have been children One traveler said a meningi
trampled when the crowd epidemic has killed thousands

FBI May End
N.J. Hunt For
More Bodies

Jackson Township,
March 25 (P)—The FBI prepared
to abandon today its first
of a suspected Cosa Nost
cemetery where two bodies w
discovered

After two days of addition
excavation proved fruitle
Richard J. Baker, FBI a
from the New York off
directed the probe, said
ury said that two unidentif

NING SUN 7 STAR ★★★★★★

Y. MARCH 25, 1967   20 Pages   10 Cents

adly Damage
cal School Lab

&Ↄ *Chapter Eight* ∝

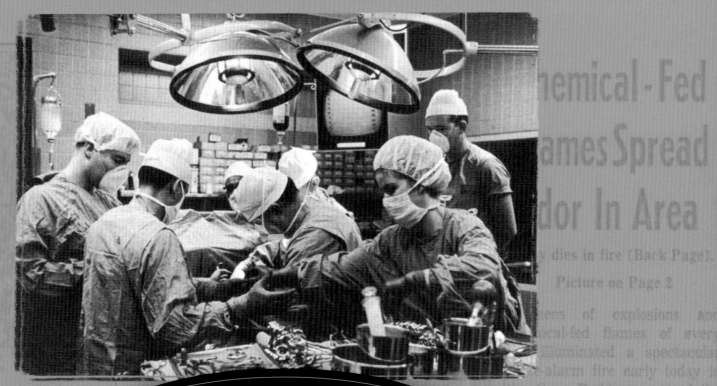

1960~1983

hemical-Fed
ames Spread
dor In Area

y dies in fire [Back Page].
                Picture on Page 2

ens   of   explosions   and
cal-fed   flames   of   every
terminated   a   spectacular
-alarm fire early today i
the Gray Building, part of th
University of Maryland Schoo
of Medicine complex at Lom
bard and Greene streets.
   More than 30 pieces of fir
equipment were called to battl
the stubborn blaze in a three
story brick building, built befor
World War I, across the stree
from University Hospital.

1960

Officials at the Social Security Administration warned of a looming crisis. A generation of elderly Americans, it cautioned, was being financially ruined by the high cost of medical care. Debates were underway in the Congress on measures to solve the problem. Five years later, the Social Security Act of 1935 would be amended to establish Medicare, a social insurance program designed to provide older adults with comprehensive health care. Medicaid would be included in the package. This companion program was designed as a joint federal/state entitlement providing medical care to primarily low-income Americans.

There was another emerging dilemma. America was graduating fewer than 8,000 physicians each year. The supply had not kept up with the country's booming population since the end of World War II. Dr. Leroy Burney, surgeon general of the Public Health Service, stated that the balance between doctors and patients in our country was "at the peril point." To maintain the present doctor/patient ratio in the year 1975, he esti-

mated that America would have to graduate 3,000 more doctors each year.

Maryland took heed of these warnings. The school had recently acquired the Hecht Building located on Redwood and Penn streets, and an appeal had been made to the U.S. Public Health Service to match state funds recently appropriated for converting the building—later renamed Howard Hall—into a suitable medical building. The structure provided Maryland with additional laboratory, classroom and study space, and Dean Stone announced that the incoming class in 1962 would be increased by as much as 25 percent. As a result, when the class graduated in 1966, there were 109 members, compared to 91 in 1965.

There was another significant addition to campus: the Health Sciences Library opened on the southeast corner of Lombard and Greene streets, across from Davidge Hall. It combined the libraries of medicine, dentistry, pharmacy, nursing, and psychiatry at a cost of $1.2 million. Stone also reported that plans for urban renewal of the Baltimore campus were moving forward. More than $4.3 million in federal funds had been made available, and matching funds from the state were being debated by the legislature.

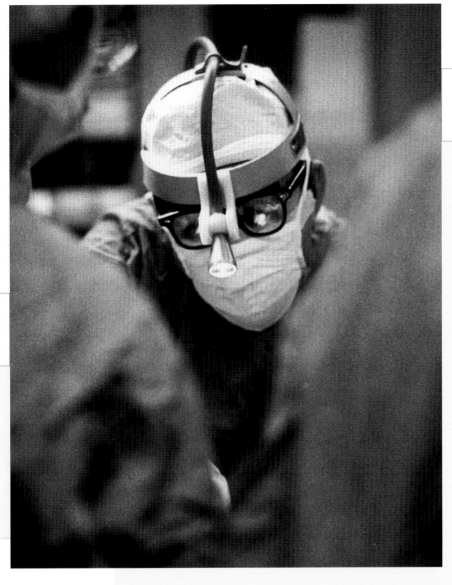

1961

so **Joseph S. McLaughlin**, class of 1956, was the first physician to describe the treatment of pulmonary alveolar proteinosis by pulmonary lavage. The advancement occurred while McLaughlin was a resident in thoracic surgery at Maryland, and the treatment was widely utilized. One year later he was the first person in the world to treat a traumatic rupture of a mitral valve by open heart surgery and plication of the valve. For 27 years, McLaughlin served as professor and head of Maryland's division of thoracic & cardiovascular surgery, and for six years he was chairman of the department of surgery.

so **Dr. Sheldon E. Greisman**, in a series of studies beginning in 1961, clarified the role of bacterial endotoxins in various febrile illnesses caused by gram negative bacteria. Specifically, in typhoid fever, Greisman showed convincingly that the clinical manifestations of the disease were not primarily attributable to circulating endotoxins but rather to the potent inflammation-inciting effect of the endotoxin elaborated at the local sites of entry by the typhoid bacillus. Greisman was elevated to professor of medicine in 1973 and professor of physiology in 1976.

so **Eugene S. Bereston**, class of 1937, team dermatologist for the Baltimore Colts and Orioles, treated New York Yankee star Roger Maris for a mysterious loss of hair. At the time Maris was attempting to break Babe Ruth's home-run record for one season, and Bereston suggested the hair loss was stress-related.

1960

so **Margaret L. Sherrard**, class of 1949, became the first female president of the Baltimore County Medical Association.

McLaughlin was the first person in the world to treat a traumatic rupture of a mitral valve by open heart surgery and plication of the valve.

1962

so **Ruth W. Baldwin**, class of 1943D, was co-discoverer of the causes of congenital cerebromacular degeneration, wherein sufferers begin losing their sight at age six or seven. She determined that the cause of the disease was hereditary, affected the kidneys, and could be chemically studied through urinary excretion. A world-renowned expert on seizure, Baldwin served for more than 25 years as head of the medical advisory board of the Maryland State Motor Vehicle Administration (MVA). Her efforts led to the MVA relaxing its policy of denying epileptics the right to drive. Beginning her career at Maryland in 1949, Baldwin established its seizure unit in the 1950s, directed its clinic for the exceptional child, and served as professor of medicine before retiring in 1987.

so The National Boxing Association changed its name to the World Boxing Association. **Leon H. Feldman**, class of 1934, was the association's chief medical officer and was responsible for writing many of the safety codes that governed boxing throughout the world.

so **Ursula T. Slager**, class of 1952, published *Space Medicine*. The textbook by this pathologist was an introduction to space medicine and served as a valuable source of information for the engineer, practicing physician, or college student receiving indoctrination into the mysteries of the space age.

Dr. Leon H. Feldman

so **Jakob E. Schmidt**, class of 1937, published the *Attorneys' Dictionary of Medicine and Word Finder*, a three-volume medical dictionary. The publication was used by attorneys, insurance companies, law enforcement agencies, and justices of the U.S. Supreme Court through more than 20 editions. Schmidt authored two dozen books over a 30-year period.

The hospital introduced its first racially integrated hospital wards.

THE WHITE HOUSE
WASHINGTON

August 23, 1963

Dear Doctor Sanislow:

Your attention and concern for Mrs. Kennedy's welfare while she was a patient at the Otis Air Force Base hospital recently was very helpful and comforting, and both of us are deeply grateful to you.

We appreciate very sincerely the dedicated efforts expended by all the members of the hospital staff, and we offer our thanks in particular for your personal contributions.

Sincerely,

Captain Charles H. Sanislow, USAF, MC
551st USAF Hospital
Otis Air Force Base
Massachusetts

1965

ℂ **George Yeager**, class of 1929 and professor of surgery, was elected director of University Hospital. Dr. Yeager served as commanding officer for Maryland's 42nd General Hospital during World War II (replacing Maurice Pincoffs), was president of the State Medical Society, and founder and editor of the new *Maryland Medical Journal*.

ℂ **Edgar R. Miller**, class of 1925, received a citation from the government of Nepal for setting up the first Christian medical network in that country. Miller, of Wilmington, Delaware, was a Methodist layman and chest surgeon. His overseas medical work included treating members of Nepal's royal family.

ℂ **Dr. Umberto VillaSanta**, Maryland professor of obstetrics and gynecology, became the first physician to warn against the use of Coumadin-like products during pregnancy. He argued that these drugs with lower molecular weight pass through the placenta and may cause hemorrhages and congenital malformations in the fetus.

1963

ℂ **Charles A. Sanislow**, class of 1956, provided medical care to President John F. Kennedy and the First Family at the summer White House in Cape Cod. This service was provided while Sanislow was serving as chief of surgery in the U.S. Air Force stationed at the 551st Hospital in Massachusetts.

For Captain Charles Sanislow — with deep appreciation

August 1963   Jacqueline Kennedy

1965

▄ **Dr. J. Edmund Bradley** retired after 17 years as chairman of the department of pediatrics and 31 years with the university. Bradley's accomplishments included being the first to observe and describe hypertension in children with Wilm's tumor. He developed a number of successful and widely used treatments for controlling epidemic viral vomiting, and he brought attention to the high incidence of lead poisoning among the lower socioeconomic groups in Baltimore City.

Dr. Frank J. Ayd, Jr.

1966

▄ **Frank J. Ayd Jr.**, class of 1945, released volume I of the *International Drug Therapy Newsletter*. It improved channels of communication between psychiatrists and pharmacologists and brought news and information about advances in psychotropic drugs. Ayd was one of the founding fathers of the American College of Neuropsychopharmacology and the Collegium Internationale Neuropsychopharmacologicum. He participated in the early trials and evaluation of chlorpromazine for the treatment of schizophrenia in America in the 1950s, as well as in trials of other phenothiazines and other drugs. He was the editor of *Ayd's Lexicon of Psychiatry, Neurology, and the Neurosciences*, widely considered to be an encyclopedia and pharmacopoeia in these fields.

▄ **Mario Garcia-Palmieri**, class of 1951, was appointed Puerto Rican Secretary of Health, a post he held until 1967. An authority in the field of cardiovascular disease, Garcia-Palmieri served as chairman of the department of medicine at the University of Puerto Rico beginning in 1968.

1967

▄ **David M. Kipnis**, class of 1951, established the need for correlating pathophysiologic mechanisms in carbohydrate abnormalities with the action of insulin to guide the management of patients with diabetes and hypoglycemia. He served as chairman of the department of medicine at the Washington University School of Medicine in St. Louis from 1972 to 1992.

▄ **Colonel James B. Nuttall**, class of 1939, was named director of the U.S. Air Force's first school of aerospace medicine located in San Antonio, Texas.

▄ A three-alarm fire caused severe damage to offices, clinics and laboratories of Gray Laboratory, a three-story building adjacent to Davidge Hall. Malfunctioning equipment in the gross anatomy lab, located in the basement, was the cause. Some 200 skeletons used for anatomy instruction were destroyed, including bones of the late Dr. Eduard Uhlenhuth, Maryland's famed anatomy professor.

The world's first Shock Trauma Center opened at Maryland for the treatment of patients suffering from traumatic injuries and shock.

1968

so The world's first Shock Trauma Center opened at Maryland for the treatment of patients suffering from traumatic injuries and shock. The director was **R Adams Cowley**, class of 1944, a pioneer in cardiac surgery. His wartime experiences in France and Germany convinced Cowley that special methods were needed to increase the survival rates of trauma victims. He developed the famous "Golden Hour" theory, the idea that there is a tiny window of opportunity when trauma victims can be saved by specially trained doctors and nurses in a properly equipped surgical setting. With the help of medical school administrators, Cowley convinced the U.S. Department of Defense and other sources to grant the necessary resources. State funding was acquired, and a U.S. Department of Transportation grant provided the first Med-Evac helicopter service. The center became a model for similar systems throughout the world.

so **Mark E. Bradley**, class of 1962, was among 54 officers, enlisted personnel and civilians selected as aquanauts for the U.S. Navy's SEALAB III, which explored the mysteries of "inner space." Bradley's experiments included a descent to more than 600 feet where he stayed for a week. The information gathered represented the most extensive body of knowledge ever collected on the effects of human living and working at very high pressures in a helium-oxygen underwater atmosphere.

so **Robert M. N. Crosby**, class of 1943D, published *The Waysiders*, one of the first books on the subject of dyslexia. A resident of Monkton, Maryland, Crosby was one of the first neurosurgeons to limit his practice exclusively to children. He was a founding member of both the International Association of Pediatric Neurosurgeons and the pediatric neurosurgical division of the American Association of Neurological Surgeons.

Dr. Mark E. Bradley

so **Selvin Passen**, class of 1960, co-founded Maryland Medical Laboratories, Inc. The clinical testing laboratory became the largest in the region and ranked seventh nationally. By the time it was sold to Corning, Inc, in 1994, the laboratory was also considered one of the most highly respected clinical laboratories in the country, not only for its diagnostic services but also for its research. Passen was an active member of the alumni association and in 1990 spearheaded an effort to establish an endowment fund to support its operating expenses which bears his name.

1969

William H. Mosberg Jr., class of 1944, created the Foundation for International Education in Neurological Surgery, Inc., an educational liaison agency for the world's neurosurgical societies. Mosberg was professor of neurological surgery at Maryland and president of the Congress of Neurological Surgeons. His studies showed that focused ultrasound produced predictable and reproducible localized destructive lesions in the central nervous system. He also reported the first case of hemorrhage resulting from trauma to the anterior choroidal artery.

Jonas R. Rappeport, class of 1952, a forensic psychiatrist, was a founder and first president of the American Academy of Psychiatry and the Law. He also served as the academy's medical director from 1981 to 1995. Rappeport testified in several high-profile criminal cases involving John Hinckley (who shot President Ronald Reagan), Sara Jane Moore (who shot at President Gerald Ford), and Arthur Bremer (who shot Alabama Gov. George Wallace).

George T. Smith, class of 1956, was named first dean at the University of Nevada School of Medicine in Reno. A renowned cardiovascular pathologist, Smith served as dean for ten years and helped expand the school from a two-year to a four-year program.

David A. Levy, class of 1954, directed and published the first randomized double-blind, placebo-controlled clinical study of allergen immunotherapy in children. It demonstrated that allergen immunotherapy, in addition to decreasing the symptoms of hay fever, also suppressed the normally occurring rise in the level of allergen-specific IgE antibody. The results were published in the *New England Journal of Medicine* and the *Journal of Clinical Investigation*. The study occurred while Levy was an assistant professor at the Johns Hopkins School of Public Health & Hygiene.

Dr. John H. Moxley III was named dean.

The University of Maryland Board of Regents approved expanding the medical school's incoming class size from 100 to 200. The increase was a response to the need for more physicians in Maryland. As a result, enrollment increased steadily and peaked in 1980 at approximately 180 students. By the 1990s, however, it was rolled back to 150.

Dr. John H. Moxley III
(Dean 1969-73)

John H. Moxley graduated from Williams College and received his medical degree from the University of Colorado. He was board certified in internal medicine, a fellow of the American College of Physicians, and a distinguished fellow of the American College of Physician Executives.

Moxley served on the dean's staff at Harvard Medical School, became dean at Maryland in 1969, and then vice chancellor for health services and dean at the University of California at San Diego. A former assistant secretary for health affairs at the U.S. Department of Defense, Moxley later consulted on organizational issues in medicine and health care. He became managing director of the physician executive practice at Korn/Ferry International, recruiting management physicians sought by private and public sectors of medicine and the health care industry.

Moxley was an active participant in several academic and health organizations. He served on the board of trustees of the American Hospital Association, as both chairman of the scientific board and member of the governing council of the California Medical Association, as member and chairman of the council of scientific affairs of the American Medical Association, and as a board member of both the National Fund for Medical Education and the Henry M. Jackson Foundation for the Advancement of Military Medicine.

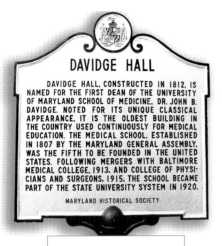

DAVIDGE HALL

DAVIDGE HALL, CONSTRUCTED IN 1812, IS NAMED FOR THE FIRST DEAN OF THE UNIVERSITY OF MARYLAND SCHOOL OF MEDICINE, DR. JOHN B. DAVIDGE. NOTED FOR ITS UNIQUE CLASSICAL APPEARANCE, IT IS THE OLDEST BUILDING IN THE COUNTRY USED CONTINUOUSLY FOR MEDICAL EDUCATION. THE MEDICAL SCHOOL, ESTABLISHED IN 1807 BY THE MARYLAND GENERAL ASSEMBLY, WAS THE FIFTH TO BE FOUNDED IN THE UNITED STATES. FOLLOWING MERGERS WITH BALTIMORE MEDICAL COLLEGE, 1913, AND COLLEGE OF PHYSICIANS AND SURGEONS, 1915, THE SCHOOL BECAME PART OF THE STATE UNIVERSITY SYSTEM IN 1920.

MARYLAND HISTORICAL SOCIETY

Davidge Hall was designated an official historical site by the Maryland Historical Trust, thanks to efforts by the Medical Alumni Association and John O. Sharrett, class of 1952. In 1974 it was entered on the National Register of Historic Places. In 1997 it was designated a National Historic Landmark by the U.S. Department of the Interior.

1970

1973

Shock Trauma converted the roof of a garage adjacent to its building into a heliport. An education program was developed for ambulance crews, and computers were installed.

Drs. **Joseph W. Burnett**, **Gary J. Calton**, and **Laure Aurelian** began investigating the sea nettle and related venomous sea animals. They showed that the animal's venom, stored in its tentacle, acted on the muscle, heart, nerves and skin. The researchers compiled all the human disorders induced by these animals, showing that most occurred by toxic mechanisms, but a few were induced by immunological pathways. Their findings were published in numerous papers and one book. As a result, verapamil was found to prevent and reverse the cardiotoxic action of these venoms. Burnett was interim chairman of the department of dermatology from 1977 until 2003.

Henry H. Bohlman, class of 1964, began his pioneering work for anterior decompressions and fusions for spinal cord injuries, which enhanced the neurologic recovery of both complete and incomplete spinal cord injuries at all levels of the spine. The first case occurred while he was a senior resident in orthopaedic surgery at Johns Hopkins, and his work continued at Case Western Reserve where he became professor of orthopaedic surgery and director of the spine institute.

1972

Dr. J. Tyson Tildon and pediatrics chairman, **Dr. Marvin Cornblath**, discovered a new children's disease known as CoA Transferase Deficiency, a central nervous system disorder. Tildon was professor of pediatrics, director of pediatric research, and the school's first associate dean for research and graduate studies.

Dr. Y.C. Lee, professor of medicine at Maryland, treated a 72-year-old man dying of heart failure with a beta-blocker. The patient had been hospitalized and was not responding to accepted treatment. According to conventional medical wisdom at the time, beta-blockers were contraindicated. But the man's condition improved as he continued taking the medication, and he lived for several more years. Lee initially received ridicule for his actions. He treated an additional seven patients with low doses of propranolol and reported his findings at an international symposium. Finally, in 1998, a landmark study co-directed at the medical school determined that adding beta-blocker therapy to standard treatment for congestive heart failure saved lives, thus vindicating Lee.

Robert Berkow, class of 1953, was appointed editor of the *Merck Manual*, the most popular medical reference in the world. First published in 1899, the manual was a compendium of causes, symptoms, treatments, and possible outcomes for virtually every medical disorder afflicting humans. Berkow held the editorial position until retirement in 2000.

William I. Wolff, class of 1940, along with a colleague at Beth Israel Medical Center in New York City, reported the use of a colonoscope, made of optical fibers, to successfully remove small growths in the colon. The new exploratory technique avoided abdominal surgery and sharply reduced recovery time for patients. His papers were published as lead articles in the *Journal of the American Medical Association* and the *New England Journal of Medicine*.

Dr. John Murray Dennis

(Dean 1973-90)

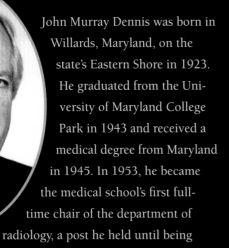

John Murray Dennis was born in Willards, Maryland, on the state's Eastern Shore in 1923. He graduated from the University of Maryland College Park in 1943 and received a medical degree from Maryland in 1945. In 1953, he became the medical school's first full-time chair of the department of radiology, a post he held until being named acting dean in 1973. Dennis was very active in organized radiology, serving as president of the American College of Radiology and chairman of its board of chancellors.

He accepted the deanship in 1974, and he added the titles of vice chancellor for health affairs in 1975 and vice president for academic affairs in 1983. During his deanship, the medical school developed into a major research institution with considerable growth in faculty and research support. After a long political battle, Dennis stewarded the development of a new Baltimore Veterans Administration Medical Center on Maryland's campus which opened in 1991. To recognize his role in bringing the VA to the Baltimore campus, the second-floor auditorium was named in his honor. Dennis was also instrumental in developing the Area Health Education Centers to expose students to rural medical practice.

When Dennis retired from the deanship in 1990, he had completed 17 years at the post and nearly 50 years of continuous service to Maryland. He was named dean emeritus in 1990 and professor emeritus in diagnostic radiology in 1995. At its 1993 commencement, the University of Maryland, Baltimore honored Dennis with an honorary ScD degree. Other honors included the American College of Radiology's gold medal for distinguished and extraordinary service, the Caldwell Medal of the American Roentgen-Ray Society, and Loyola College's Andrew White Medal for distinguished service to Maryland. ཉ

1973

ཉ **John M. Dennis**, class of 1945, was named dean.

ཉ **Mathew H. M. Lee**, class of 1956, was one of 12 American medical scholars invited by Chairman Mao Tse Tung to visit the People's Republic of China, where Lee studied acupuncture analgesia for the treatment of pain. Lee became one of America's leading authorities on rehabilitation medicine, serving as the Howard A. Rusk Professor of Rehabilitative Medicine at NYU School of Medicine beginning in 1997 and chairman of the department in 1998. He also held professorships in NYU schools of dentistry and music where he conducted additional research.

ཉ **Robert O. Hickman**, class of 1957, while doing consultation work with the Fred Hutchinson Cancer

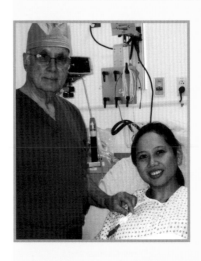

Research Center in Seattle, invented the Hickman catheter. The long, thin tube made of flexible silicone rubber had as many as three openings and was used to deliver multiple drug regimens to bone marrow transplant patients in virtually every cancer center in the world. Hickman's innovation was the culmination of a career dedicated to advancing central venous access. In 1960, as a first-year fellow in nephrology at the University of Washington, Hickman served on a team that placed the world's first patient on long-term hemodialysis.

1974

1975

ᔍ **Dr. Michael A. Berman** developed the Berman angiographic catheter that was widely used in pediatric cardiac diagnosis. Berman was chairman of pediatrics from 1984 to 1997.

Dr. Myron M. Levine

ᔍ A clinical research center for vaccine development was established by **Drs. Richard B. Hornick** and **Myron M. Levine**, providing facilities where new vaccines could be evaluated in community volunteers, a novel concept in that era. Two years later, in 1976, under Dr. Levine's directorship, the University of Maryland Center for Vaccine Development (CVD) was founded, as its work-scope was greatly expanded to include basic vaccine research and epidemiologic field activities in developing countries. The first CVD field site was established in Santiago, Chile, in 1979, in conjunction with the Chilean Ministry of Health. From 1979 until 1990, the CVD carried out four large-scale field trials of a live oral typhoid vaccine in 465,000 Chilean schoolchildren that demonstrated the safety and efficacy of the vaccine and led to its approval by the FDA. In 1994, a genetically-engineered single-dose live oral cholera vaccine strain developed and tested by Levine and **Dr. James Kaper** was licensed in several countries. It was used by the World Health Organization to control a cholera epidemic in Micronesia six years later. By 2004, the CVD celebrated 30 years of leadership as the world's largest and most diverse academic vaccine development enterprise. Its staff managed an array of basic research laboratories and clinical trial facilities in Baltimore, South America, and in two locations in Africa in pursuit of vaccines for enteric infections, lower respiratory infections, malaria, invasive bacterial infections, and measles.

ᔍ **Maurice M. Reeder**, class of 1958, co-authored *Gamuts in Radiology*, the first reliable text dealing with differential diagnosis. He was chairman of the department of radiology at the University of Hawaii from 1978 to 1997.

1976

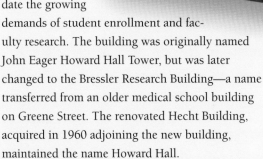

ᔍ A new 14-story building located on Baltimore Street opened to accommodate the growing demands of student enrollment and faculty research. The building was originally named John Eager Howard Hall Tower, but was later changed to the Bressler Research Building—a name transferred from an older medical school building on Greene Street. The renovated Hecht Building, acquired in 1960 adjoining the new building, maintained the name Howard Hall.

ᔍ **Enrique Perez-Santiago**, class of 1943M, was named dean of the University of Puerto Rico Medical School, holding the post until 1978. Perez-Santiago, professor of medicine at the university, was recognized by colleagues as the "father of Puerto Rican hematology."

1977

Dean Moxley taking a ride with Dr. Goldberg

🔊 **David J. Shiling** and **Nelson H. Goldberg**, members of the class of 1973, while training at the National Institutes of Health, devised, authored and initiated the first prospective randomized government-sponsored studies to evaluate the use of marijuana as an anti-emetic for patients receiving chemotherapy. Results of the study, demonstrating a reduction in vomiting and retching episodes for those using marijuana, appeared in *Annals of Internal Medicine* in 1979 and in *Cancer* in 1980.

🔊 The Medical Alumni Association incorporated and announced a $1.5 million campaign to restore the interior of Davidge Hall. The project was completed in 1982.

1978

The nation's first state-wide Emergency Medical System telecommunications system was installed, linking 20 specialty referral centers, 51 hospital emergency departments, a fleet of state police Med-Evac helicopters, and more than 300 ambulance companies.

1979

Guyther at the White House with Roslyn Carter

🔊 **J. Roy Guyther**, class of 1943D, was named family doctor of the year by the American Academy of Family Physicians and was honored at a White House ceremony. Guyther was associate professor of family medicine at Maryland.

🔊 **Charles C. Edwards**, class of 1968 and professor and chief of orthopaedic surgery at Maryland, along with his colleagues introduced adjustable external fixation to the treatment of open fractures and major orthopaedic trauma in North America. Concurrently, Edwards refined spinal instrumentation by developing the rod-sleeve method to improve spine alignment and reduce surgical failures in the treatment of spinal fractures. His new spine tumor procedures enabled total resection of the sacrum and lower lumbar vertebrae and brought international publicity to Maryland. In the mid to late 1980s, Edwards developed the first modular spinal instrumentation. It introduced both sacral screw fixation for spinal rods and three-dimensional vertebral adjustability. This enabled Edwards to pioneer the concept of gradual reduction of chronic spinal deformities by means of stress relaxation.

1980

🔊 The Sudden Infant Death Syndrome Institute opened at Maryland. It was the nation's first institute to combine research, education, and patient care into a comprehensive study of what is commonly known as SIDS or crib death. The institute was supported by a $2.8 million grant from the National Institute for Child Health and Human Development.

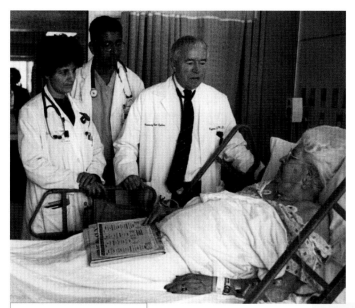

Dr. Bahr *(standing right)* making rounds.

1981

∞ **Frederick "Fritz" W. Plugge IV**, class of 1957, was commander of the U.S. Air Force Hospital in Wiesbaden, Germany, which received 52 American hostages released by Iranian militants after 444 days in captivity. Plugge, a surgeon, retired with the rank of brigadier general. To express his appreciation to Maryland for the exemplary education and training he received, Plugge endowed three faculty positions in the department of surgery.

∞ **Raymond D. Bahr**, class of 1962, opened the world's first chest pain center in the emergency department at St. Agnes Hospital in Baltimore. Bahr and his collaborators studied the effects of early intervention on patients experiencing chest pain.

1983

∞ **Augustus Frye Jr.**, class of 1943D, developed a "slider" knot technique for arthroscopic shoulder surgery that became known as the Tennessee Slider. The orthopaedic surgeon practicing in Lookout Mountain, Tennessee, began searching for an effective method after recognizing the difficulty in tying a knot inside a joint.

∞ **Dr. Leonard S. Taylor**, a faculty member in the department of radiation oncology who held a joint appointment as professor of electrical engineering at the University of Maryland College Park, teamed up with medical engineers to develop a microwave scalpel. About the size of a normal surgical knife, the scalpel controlled bleeding more efficiently during critical operations.

∞ **Walter J. Wiechetek**, class of 1972 and an aerospace physician at Hamilton Standard, designed a patch for space suits of NASA astronauts. The multi-colored patch was adapted from a Leonardo da Vinci sketch entitled *The Dimensions of Man*. It depicted a 15th century man wearing a space outfit and three stars honoring fallen astronauts.

Chapter Nine

1984~2007

1984

aryland's hospital was struggling. For years its state subsidy had been shrinking. Changing conditions in the healthcare field were also threatening its solvency and jeopardizing its mission of offering quality specialty care as well as comprehensive medical care to the community.

Since 1977, separating the hospital from the state and university system had been discussed by the appropriations committee of the Maryland House of Delegates. Why should the state maintain a mere administrative affiliation with the hospital if it had no vested financial interest? The chancellor for the Baltimore campus, **Dr. T. Albert Farmer**, agreed. Allowing the hospital to function as an independent institution, he suggested, would grant it greater flexibility and efficiency.

Dr. T. Albert Farmer

Legislation was introduced during the spring legislative session, and on April 9 a bill creating a private, not-for-profit hospital complex known as University of Maryland Medical System (UMMS) was signed into law by Governor Harry Hughes. In a strange twist of fate, it was on this same day that Farmer died suddenly in his home. He was 52 years old and had been chancellor since 1981.

Hughes appointed a 21-member board of directors responsible for the system's governance. **Morton I. Rapoport**, class of 1960, medical school associate dean and head of the hospital since 1982, became chief executive officer.

Who was responsible for management of the doctors, and how would state employees and their entitlements be dealt with in this new private corporation? The plan called for all hospital physicians to be recognized as medical school faculty members. Non-faculty employees were given the opportunity to continue as state employees or become members of the new corporation, but new personnel would automatically become employees of the corporation.

Dr. Morton I. Rapoport

Under Rapoport's leadership, the system quickly eliminated its annual million dollar deficits. Before his retirement in 2003, it would grow into a six-hospital organization consisting of the University of Maryland Medical Center, Baltimore Washington Medical Center, Maryland General Hospital, Kernan Hospital, University Specialty Hospital (formerly Deaton Hospital), and Mt. Washington Pediatric Hospital. Admissions soared from 19,000 in 1984 to 60,000 in 2003, with revenues increasing from $165 million to $1 billion during this same period. As the medical system began to grow to include other hospitals, the former University Hospital became known as the University of Maryland Medical Center (UMMC).

1984

so **Dr. A. Avinoam Kowarski**, director of the division of pediatric endocrinology, reported in the *Journal of the American Medical Association* that Maryland had developed a test which accurately diagnosed idiopathic post-prandial syndrome, a condition characterized by a drop in blood sugar commonly known as reactive hypoglycemia. Maryland faculty contributors included **Stuart Chalew**, class of 1977; **Judith McLaughlin**, class of 1972; **Drs. James Mersey; Anthony Adams**; and **Marvin Cornblath**.

1985

so **Morton M. Mower**, class of 1959, co-invented the implantable automatic defibrillator which received approval by the FDA. The device monitored and, if necessary, corrected abnormal heart rhythms. Mower was a cardiologist at Baltimore's Sinai Hospital and began working on the device with Dr. Michel Mirowski in 1969. During his career Mower received 26 patents.

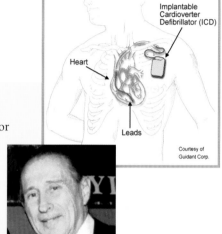

so **John C. Blasko**, class of 1969, a radiation oncologist, and a small team of physicians established a minimally-invasive technique utilizing brachytherapy for treatment of prostate cancer. It became a standard treatment, resulting in long-term survival rates similar to those undergoing radical prostatectomy. The group founded the Seattle Prostate Institute.

Dr. John C. Blasko

so **Carol Lee Koski**, class of 1968 and professor of neurology, made her initial observations of complement fixing antibodies to myelin in the serum of patients with paralysis caused by the Guillain-Barré Syndrome.

1986

A 24-member team at Maryland led by Dr. J. Laurance Hill, professor and head of pediatric surgery, successfully separated two-month-old conjoined twins. The surgery was videotaped and proved to be an excellent teaching tool for another Maryland team performing the same procedure in 2002.

The nation's first use of supported angioplasty to open blocked arteries took place at Maryland.

1988

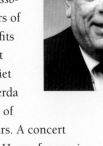

🙦 **James J. Cerda**, class of 1961, published "The Role of Grapefruit Pectin in Health and Disease" in *Transactions of the American Clinical and Climatological Association*. The paper summarized 20 years of investigation into the nutritional benefits of citrus pectin. Cerda determined that adding grapefruit pectin to the daily diet lowered blood levels of cholesterol. Cerda served on the faculty of the University of Florida College of Medicine for 28 years. A concert pianist, Cerda performed at the White House for presidents Truman, Eisenhower, and Kennedy.

🙦 **Israel Weiner**, class of 1953, was named first chairman of the Maryland State Board of Physician Quality Assurance. The position was created as a result of a merger between the state's physician licensing board and the medical disciplinary agency. Weiner, a neurosurgeon, served two terms as chair.

1987

🙦 The Davidge mace was presented to the Medical Alumni Association by **Celeste L.** and **Theodore E. Woodward**, members of the class of 1938. The sterling silver mace was cast in Mexico, and the wooden staff was crafted by Steve Davies, a cabinetmaker and hospital employee. The piece was an exact replica of Davidge Hall and would take part in all future medical school ceremonies.

🙦 The nation's first use of supported angioplasty to open blocked arteries took place at Maryland. The procedure, in which patients were connected to a heart-lung machine, provided a safe alternative for people too weak to undergo traditional balloon angioplasty or bypass surgery. The procedure was administered by **Drs. Robert A. Vogel**, head of the division of cardiology and **Steven R. Gundry Jr.**, of the division of thoracic surgery. Maryland also served as the headquarters for the Registry of Supported Angioplasty, where data on the procedure were collected and analyzed.

1989

🙦 The plastic surgery divisions at Maryland and Johns Hopkins formed a single, shared residency training program, the first combined plastic surgery training program between two medical institutions. They came together under the leadership of **Nelson H. Goldberg**, class of 1973, and professor and chief of plastic and reconstructive surgery.

1989

℠ The new R Adams Cowley Shock Trauma Center building received its first patients in January. Located at Lombard and Penn streets, the 11-level facility opened at a cost of $41 million. The facility included a rooftop heliport capable of accommodating up to four Med-Evac helicopters.

℠ Two Maryland general surgeons—**Dr. Karl Zucker**, associate professor of surgery, and **Dr. Robert Bailey**, assistant professor of surgery—performed the first minimally invasive gall bladder removal in the Northeastern U.S. using a laparoscope with a tiny video camera attached. Only three small holes were required to complete the procedure, compared to the standard 8-10 inch incision, meaning less pain and a much faster recovery time for patients. They trained surgeons in this procedure and worked with surgical equipment makers to adapt their instruments to this new type of surgery. Among them was the *Maryland Retractor*, a standard laparoscopic surgical tool.

1990

℠ **Dr. Richard D. Richards**, professor and head of the department of ophthalmology, was named acting dean.

℠ **Richard F. Leighton**, class of 1955, was appointed vice president for academic affairs and dean of the school of medicine at the Medical College of Ohio at Toledo, a position he held until 1996. Leighton joined the institution in 1974 as a professor of medicine and chief of the division of cardiology.

1991

℠ **Dr. Donald E. Wilson** was named dean.

Dr. Donald E. Wilson
(Dean 1991–2006)

Donald E. Wilson, a native of Worcester, Massachusetts, was a graduate of Harvard University and Tufts University School of Medicine. Appointed dean in 1991, he became vice president for medical affairs in 1999. Wilson came to Maryland after 11 years as professor and chairman of medicine at the State University of New York Health Science Center-Brooklyn, and physician-in-chief of the University Hospital of Brooklyn and Kings County Hospital Center in New York.

As dean, Wilson reformed the curriculum, providing students with a broad correlation of basic science and clinical medicine at the outset of their medical education. Wilson was recognized locally and nationally as a champion for increasing the number of under-represented minorities among both students and faculty.

Under Wilson's leadership, the medical school climbed to the top tier of American medical institutions in research funding. His policy expertise led to his appointment as chair of the state's Health Care Access and Cost Commission and, subsequently, the renamed Maryland Health Care Commission. Wilson served as chairman of the Association of American Medical Colleges for 2003–04, was a member of the national advisory council on research resources of the NIH, and was named to the advisory committee of the NIH director.

A master of the American College of Physicians, his memberships also included the Institute of Medicine of the National Academy of Sciences, the American Clinical and Climatological Association and Alpha Omega Alpha. He was a founder of the Association for Academic Minority Physicians. ℠

The Baltimore VA Medical Center

1992

80 **Philip A. Mackowiak**, class of 1970, in the *Journal of the American Medical Association*, showed that the longtime standard for body temperature—98.6F—was inaccurate. His research refuted the century-old belief developed by German physician Carl Wunderlich. Mackowiak demonstrated that normal body temperature averages 98.2F, but it can fluctuate during the day, and there are variances with regard to age, gender, and even race. A professor of medicine and amateur

medical historian, Mackowiak developed an annual historical clinicopathological conference at Maryland in 1995. The program was devoted to the modern medical diagnosis of disorders that affected prominent historical figures.

1991

80 **Drs. Mordecai P. Blaustein** and **John M. Hamlyn** discovered a new hormone that plays a key role in hypertension. Working with scientists at the Upjohn Company, they purified, from human plasma, a new adrenocortical hormone indistinguishable from the plant compound, ouabain, a cardiotonic steroid. Plasma levels of endogenous ouabain are elevated in half of all humans with essential hypertension. Blaustein was professor and chairman of the department of physiology at Maryland, where Hamlyn was a professor.

80 **Allen R. Myers**, class of 1960, was named dean of the Temple University School of Medicine, a post he held through 1995. An international authority in the management of scleroderma and other connective-tissue diseases, Myers joined Temple in 1978. From 2000 to 2002, he served as president of the Philadelphia College of Physicians.

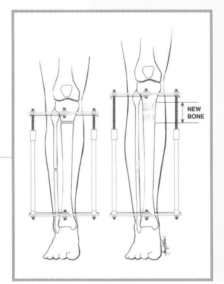

NEW BONE

80 Maryland announced the establishment of the limb lengthening and reconstruction center. The center featured **Drs. Dror Paley** and **John Herzenberg**, associate professors of orthopaedic surgery, who were recognized as the country's most experienced physicians using the Ilizarov bone lengthening method.

The Baltimore VA Medical Center opened on the northwest corner of Baltimore and Greene streets. It featured the world's first filmless radiology department. The Baltimore VA soon rose from 26th to number one in research funds among the nation's 132 veterans establishments.

1992

A new hyperbaric chamber was delivered to Maryland's R Adams Cowley Shock Trauma Center. One of the largest in the country, the chamber allowed for the treatment of up to 20 patients at one time for carbon monoxide poisoning, smoke inhalation, burns, gas gangrene, and crush injuries as well as decompression sickness and air embolism caused by scuba diving. Patients with diabetic ulcers, chronic osteomyelitis, and those suffering from the chronic side effects of radiation therapy also received treatment from the new chamber.

1994

 Reforms were brought to the educational curriculum. Lecture time for the first-year class was reduced from eight hours per day to two. Instruction was presented in blocks—varying in length—with small-group teaching, problem-based learning, and increased time for self-study. Basic sciences became multi-disciplinary with emphasis on their clinical relevance. During the clinical years a stronger emphasis was placed on education in the ambulatory setting. Computer labs were built in Howard Hall, and each student was equipped with a laptop computer. The incoming class of 1998 became the country's first medical class required to take informatics training as part of the curriculum. The effort was headed by the vice dean, **Dr. Frank M. Calia**.

1993

 One hundred fifty years after his death, the Medical Alumni Association placed a marker at the grave of **Dr. Nathaniel Potter** in Greenmount Cemetery. From 1826 until 1839, Potter fought the state to return control of the University of Maryland to its independent board of regents. The legal battles to accomplish this depleted Potter's fortune, and he was buried in an unmarked grave.

 Dr. Kenneth P. Johnson, professor and chairman of the department of neurology beginning in 1980 and director of the Maryland Center for Multiple Sclerosis, was key investigator in a clinical trial that led to FDA approval of Betaseron—the first drug ever approved specifically to treat MS by reducing the number of attacks and delaying the natural course of the disease. Johnson was recognized for his leadership in designing and testing new treatments for MS as well as his pioneering laboratory work to identify an infectious trigger of the disease. He led testing of Copaxone, another drug approved by the FDA, to slow the progression of the disease.

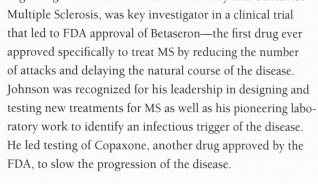

1994

20-Year Tuition Comparison		
Year	In-State Residents	Out-of-State Residents
1974	$1,070	$2,170
1984	$3,929	$7,322
1994	$10,751	$20,851

☙ The medical center's Homer Gudelsky Building opened on the northwest corner of Lombard and Greene streets. The 12-story facility housed cancer care, neurocare, cardiac care, transplant surgery, diagnostic imaging, and a radiation oncology program. The building, with its sky-lit atrium, honored the memory of Homer Gudelsky, a prominent Maryland businessman and philanthropist who was treated at the cancer center.

☙ **Dr. Eve J. Higginbotham** became the first woman in America to chair a university-based department of ophthalmology when she came to Maryland. Higginbotham was the first author of a paper demonstrating the benefits of topical medical therapy in either delaying the onset or preventing the development of glaucoma among African Americans with ocular hypertension. She co-edited four textbooks in the field of ophthalmology, was elected to the Institute of Medicine in 2000 and, six years later, became dean of the Morehouse School of Medicine in Atlanta.

☙ **J. Stephen Dumler**, class of 1985 and assistant professor of pathology at Maryland, was among a team of scientists who identified a new and sometimes fatal bacterial disease spread by a tick bite. In an article published in the *Journal of the American Medical Association*, they reported the confirmation of 12 cases of Human Granulocytic Ehrlichiosis. Unlike other tick-borne diseases, its skin rashes were not a common symptom.

☙ At age 51, **Gail Fredericks** became the medical school's oldest graduate at commencement ceremonies.

☙ **Ronn Wade**, director of Maryland's anatomical services division and head of the Maryland State Anatomy Board, mummified a human body using the exact tools and techniques of the ancient Egyptians. It was the first mummification in more than 3,000 years and would be compared to other preserved bodies to measure changes over time. The event was recorded and broadcast in a *National Geographic* documentary.

Dr. James Frenkil and wife Carolyn McGuire Frenkil

1995

☙ Health Sciences Facility I opened on Pine Street. The six-story facility featured 86 thousand square feet of space designated for scientific research. Projects included the search for an AIDS vaccine, new treatments for neurobiological diseases, cancer, and the search for improved therapies for heart disease and hypertension. Health Sciences Facility II would follow in 2003.

☙ A unique collaboration between Maryland neurosurgeon **Walker L. Robinson**, class of 1970, and dentists **Gary D. Hack and Richard T. Koritzer** resulted in the discovery of connective tissue at the skull base not previously described in medical literature. The tissue forms a bridge between the deep neck muscles and the dura mater, the membrane that covers the brain and spinal cord. The researchers speculated that when neck muscles contract, the connective tissue bridge tenses and pulls on the dura mater, causing the pain of tension headaches. Robinson observed that when these tissues were severed, previously unexplained contraction headaches disappeared.

Drs. Walker L. Robinson and Gary D. Hack

☙ The Frenkil Building opened on Eutaw Street. The building was donated by **James Frenkil**, class of 1937, and wife Carolyn McGuire-Frenkil to house several ambulatory services including otolaryngology and neurology practices, general medicine, and the infectious disease clinic. Dr. Frenkil's specialty was occupational medicine.

1995

The incoming class of 1999, consisting of 150 students, was selected from a record 4,700 applications, most in the school's history.

1996

ɞ The Institute of Human Virology opened on Lombard Street. Headed by **Dr. Robert C. Gallo**, the institute brought together the fields of basic science, clinical research, epidemiology and prevention, animal models, and vaccine studies in the pursuit of breakthroughs in the battle against AIDS and other viral diseases. Gallo was credited with discovering two leukemia viruses and co-discovering the HIV virus that causes AIDS.

ɞ The Ravens, Baltimore's new NFL team, chose Maryland's University Sports Medicine to provide comprehensive care for its players. University Sports Medicine also cared for the varsity athletic programs at the University of Maryland College Park.

ɞ For the first time in the history of the medical school, the graduating class consisted of a female majority.

ɞ **Drs. Stephen T. Bartlett** and **Stephen C. Jacobs** initiated the laparoscopic living kidney donor program at Maryland, and within a few years it became the largest in the world. The technique supplanted open surgery as the standard for kidney removal, and the medical center became an international training site for the procedure. They completed their 1,000th laparoscopic kidney removal in 2005—the world's first hospital to achieve this milestone. Bartlett served as chairman of the department of surgery, and Jacobs was a professor of surgery.

ɞ **Louis R. Caplan**, class of 1962, published a monograph on posterior circulation strokes, a classic in the field. Caplan was chief of cardiovascular diseases at Beth Israel Deaconess Hospital in Boston and professor of Neurology at Harvard. His 2004 article in the *New England Medical Center Posterior Circulation Registry* was the most complete clinical description of the varieties and outcomes of this condition.

1997

ɞ **Michael B. A. Oldstone**, class of 1961, received the J. Allyn Taylor International Prize in Medicine for his work on host:virus interrelationships—specifically for uncovering mechanisms of the way viruses persist, cause disease, and can be cleared from the infected host using immunocytotherapy. Oldstone was professor at The Scripps Research Institute in LaJolla, California where he directed the viral-immunobiology laboratory.

Dr. Stephen T. Bartlett

1998

The University of Maryland Baltimore Health Sciences and Human Services Library opened on the southwest corner of Lombard and Greene streets. The six-floor facility featured reference and circulation services as well as database and networking information. Housed in the Woodward Historical Suite on the library's top floor were books of **Dr. John Crawford**, whose collection started Maryland's library in 1815.

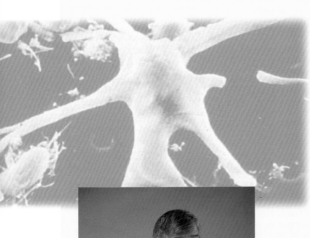

Maryland researchers published the first peer-reviewed scientific documentation of a clinical syndrome resulting from exposure to the toxins produced by Pfiesteria and Pfiesteria-like Dinoflagellates. The findings were reported in *The Lancet*. **Dr. J. Glenn Morris Jr.**, professor of medicine, epidemiology and preventive medicine at Maryland, headed a state-appointed medical team to examine people who complained of symptoms after exposure to Pfiesteria-infested waters. During August 1997, massive fish kills associated with Pfiesteria occurred in Maryland waterways, and people having contact with the water reported a variety of symptoms including fatigue, headaches, respiratory irritation, diarrhea, weight loss, skin rashes, and memory problems.

2000

Dr. Carol O. Tacket, professor of medicine at Maryland, successfully tested a potato-based vaccine to combat the Norwalk Virus, spread by contaminated food and water. The new approach to deliver a vaccine through a plant was pioneered at Maryland's center for vaccine development and Cornell University.

Medical school filmmakers **Susan Hannah Hadary** and **William Whiteford** won an Academy Award for *King Gimp*, a documentary chronicling the struggles and triumphs of a Baltimore youth growing up with cerebral palsy. Fourteen years in the making, the film won the Oscar for best short documentary.

espite exhaustive efforts by the university to keep it healthy, the Davidge Elm succumbed to age and disease and was removed. The English elm was planted in 1812 when construction of the medical school building was completed.

2001

2002

2003

Following the terrorist attacks on the World Trade Center, the Pentagon, and in Pennsylvania on September 11, 2001, Maryland's center for vaccine development was asked to measure the effectiveness of the existing stores of smallpox vaccine and determine whether the current supply could be effectively diluted in order to make more available doses. Researchers were also tapped by the NIH to evaluate a new anthrax vaccine which used part of a specific gene to create protective antibodies. In this same year, the U.S. Air Force signed an agreement with Maryland for its personnel to receive special training at the R Adams Cowley Shock Trauma Center. In 2003, Maryland received a $42 million grant to lead the regional center of excellence for biodefense and emerging infectious diseases research. The award from the National Institute of Allergy and Infectious Diseases was used to develop new and improved vaccines, diagnostic tools and treatments to help protect the country and world from the threat of bioterrorism and naturally occurring infectious diseases. In 2005, the school received a $46 million federal contract to oversee testing of medications that could be used to treat people exposed to potentially lethal doses of radiation in the event of a nuclear terrorist attack. **Dr. Thomas MacVittie**, professor of radiation oncology and pathology, received the five-year contract from the National Institute of Allergy and Infectious Diseases.

Traditional first aid measures for victims of poisonous snakebites were strongly discouraged in an article in the *New England Journal of Medicine*. The authors, **Dr. Robert A. Barish** and **Barry S. Gold**, class of 1974, argued that incision and suction, or applying a tourniquet or ice probably did more harm than good. They suggested that victims be immediately transported to the nearest medical facility to fight the potentially fatal poison. Barish, director of Maryland's division of emergency medicine, became full professor and vice dean for clinical affairs. Gold was a clinical assistant professor of medicine.

Catherine N. Smoot-Haselnus, class of 1985, an ophthalmologist from Salisbury, Maryland, became the first female president of the Maryland State Medical Society.

Taylor Manor Hospital was sold to Sheppard Pratt Health System. The psychiatric hospital was purchased in 1939 by Ellicott City businessman Isaac Taylor and his son **Irving Tayor**, class of 1943M. Over the years the younger Taylor developed one of the most progressive and reputable psychiatric hospitals on the East Coast. In 1953, Taylor Manor became the first hospital to use the drug Thorazine to treat patients, and in 1966 launched the state's first psychiatric hospital treatment program for adolescents. The institution developed a reputation for its annual symposium which attracted researchers from around the world.

Following a national directive by the Accreditation Council for Graduate Medical Education, Maryland reduced the resident work schedule to 80 duty hours per week.

Dr. Catherine N. Smoot-Haselnus

2003

ഔ In order to save the life of a woman with a rare recurring heart tumor, cardiac surgeons at Maryland's medical center performed a first-of-its-kind operation by completely removing the tumor from both of the heart's upper chambers, then reconstructing the chamber with specially treated animal and human donor tissue. To make this possible, the woman's heart was removed from her chest for several hours prior to being re-implanted. The 12-hour surgery was performed by **Dr. Bartley P. Griffith**, professor and head of the division of cardiac surgery, and **Dr. James S. Gammie**, assistant professor.

ഔ **Sara F. Goldkind**, class of 1983, became the first bioethicist appointed at the Food and Drug Administration. Her position was designed to ensure that children used in research studies by pharmaceutical companies would not be harmed in the experiments.

ഔ **Dr. Alessio Fasano**, head of Maryland's center for celiac research and mucosal biology research center, concluded the largest epidemiological study on the disorder ever conducted in the United States, with more than 13,000 subjects screened. The study showed that celiac disease affects as many as one percent of the population. Published in the *Archives of Internal Medicine*, the results contributed to the approval of a food labeling bill mandated by the FDA.

ഔ **Edmond F. Notebaert** was named president and chief executive officer of UMMS, replacing the retiring Morton I. Rapoport. Notebaert had held a similar position at Children's Hospital of Philadelphia as well as top executive positions with the Cleveland Clinic Foundation and Hospital.

2004

ഔ **June K. Robinson**, class of 1974, was named editor of *Archives of Dermatology*, the leading clinical journal in the field of dermatology. A nationally regarded skin cancer expert, Robinson was director of the division of dermatology at Loyola University Chicago and later chief of dermatology at Dartmouth Hitchcock Medical Center in Lebanon, N.H.

ഔ **Harry C. Knipp**, class of 1976, became the first chairman of the Maryland Board of Physicians. The 21-member board, appointed by the governor, was responsible for licensing all state physicians and allied health practitioners as well as imposing disciplinary measures. It replaced the Board of Physician Quality Assurance. At the end of 2003, there were 23,101 physicians with Maryland licenses.

ഔ **Herbert Spiegel**, class of 1939, published a second edition of *Trance and Treatment: Clinical Uses of Hypnosis*. A member of the faculty at the College of Physicians and Surgeons at Columbia University, Spiegel developed the Hypnotic Induction Profile, a scale useful in determining hypnosis potential. He also pioneered the use of hypnosis to effectively treat habit problems such as smoking.

ഔ Two Maryland researchers—**Drs. Brian Berman**, professor and director of Maryland's center for integrative medicine, and **Marc Hochberg**, professor and head of the division of rheumatology—published the largest randomized controlled trial in acupuncture ever conducted in America. The study, funded by the National Institutes of Health and published in the *Annals of Internal Medicine*, showed acupuncture to be a safe and effective adjunctive treatment to decrease pain and improve physical function in patients with osteoarthritis of the knee.

ഔ **Willarda V. Edwards**, class of 1977, a Baltimore internist, became the first female African-American president of the Maryland State Medical Society. She served as president and chief operating officer of the Sickle Cell Association of America and was the first to serve concurrently as president of the Baltimore chapters of the American Medical Association and National Medical Association.

2005

Fearing a pandemic, the National Institute of Allergy and Infectious Diseases asked Maryland's center for vaccine development to test an avian flu vaccine. The principal investigator of the study was **Dr. James Campbell**, assistant professor of pediatrics.

The university opened the first of a planned 10-building, $350 million biomedical research park. Located west of Martin Luther King Jr. Boulevard, the BioPark offered five acres of space for research labs, offices, and parking. It provided opportunities for collaboration between university researchers and private biopharmaceutical and life sciences companies. The effort was initiated by UMB president **David J. Ramsay**.

Maryland researchers demonstrated for the first time that laughter is linked to healthy function of blood vessels. The principal investigator was **Dr. Michael Miller**, associate professor of medicine, whose research showed that laughter appeared to cause the tissue forming the inner lining of blood vessels—the endothelium—to dilate or expand and thus increase blood flow. The magnitude of the expansion was similar to that experienced during aerobic activity. It also showed that under mental stress, the blood vessel lining developed a potentially unhealthy response reducing blood flow.

2006

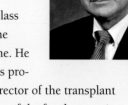

Robert M. Mentzer Jr., class of 1971, was named dean of Wayne State University School of Medicine. He joined Wayne State after serving as professor and chairman of surgery, director of the transplant center, and president and chairman of the faculty practice plan at the University of Kentucky College of Medicine.

An eight year, $4 million restoration project was completed on the exterior of Davidge Hall. The work included repointing brick, refurbishing doors and windows, and replacing the surfaces of roofing on both the gable roof and dome. The project was jointly funded by the state, a federal grant, and private support from the Medical Alumni Association.

Melvin Sharoky, class of 1976 and president and CEO of Somerset Pharmaceuticals, received FDA approval for EMSAM (selegiline transdermal system), the first transdermal patch for the treatment of major depressive disorder.

Dr. Angela H. Brodie, professor of pharmacology & experimental therapeutics at Maryland and an internationally recognized cancer researcher, received the 2006 Dorothy P. Landon American Association for Cancer Research Prize for Translational Research. One year earlier

she became the first female recipient of the Charles F. Kettering Prize in Research. The awards recognized her work in creating the first selective aromatase inhibitor—Formestane— to be used to treat breast cancer patients. Her discovery led to the development of a new class of drugs used to prevent recurrence of breast cancer in postmenopausal women. The drugs reduced the level of estrogen produced by the body, thereby cutting off the fuel that promotes the growth of cancer cells. Brodie joined Maryland's faculty in 1979.

Dr. E. Albert Reece was named vice president for medical affairs and dean.

Dr. E. Albert Reece

(Dean 2006–)

A native of Jamaica, West Indies, E. Albert Reece earned a medical degree from New York University School of Medicine in 1978. He joined Maryland in 2006 after serving for five years as vice chancellor and dean at the University of Arkansas College of Medicine in Little Rock. During this time he also served as professor in the departments of obstetrics/gynecology, medicine, and biochemistry and molecular biology.

In addition to his medical degree, Reece received a PhD in biochemistry from the University of the West Indies in Kingston, and an MBA from the Fox School of Business & Management at Temple University. His specialty and subspecialty were OB/GYN and maternal/fetal medicine, respectively, and he was an expert on the mechanism of diabetes-induced birth defects. Reece and his group of researchers discovered the dominant biochemical and molecular mechanisms underlying the cause of these defects and developed methods to prevent them. He published 11 books, four monographs, as well as 450 articles, chapters, and abstracts.

Reece served for ten years as chair of the department of obstetrics & gynecology at Temple University prior to his appointment at Arkansas. Earlier, he held appointments as clinical instructor, assistant professor and associate professor at Yale University School of Medicine. He was a member of the Institute of Medicine of the National Academy of Sciences and served on several governmental and civic organizations and committees including the FDA, IOM, NIH, and the Secretary of Health & Human Services committee on infant mortality. ◐

2006

◐ A major expansion of the medical center was completed with the opening of the top three floors of the Weinberg Building on Lombard Street with new units for intensive care, cardiac surgery, and acute surgery. Also included in the facility were 19 operating rooms and emergency departments for adults and children.

2007

◐ **The University of Maryland School of Medicine**

1,401 Faculty
1,350 Staff
  25 Academic Departments
   7 Programs
   6 Organized Research Centers
1,265 Students
  • 602 MD
  • 38 MD/PhD
  • 327 Graduate
  • 12 Master's in Genetic Counseling
  • 71 Medical & Research Technology
  • 203 Physical Therapy
  • 12 Master's in Public Health
 428 Post-doctoral fellows
 747 Residents

$19,800 Tuition for in-state MD students
$36,000 Tuition for out-of-state MD students
$350 million in Research Awards (FY05)

Bibliography

A Cyclopedia of American Medical Biography, by Howard A. Kelly, M.D., 1912, W. B. Saunders Company

A Retrospect of Surgery in Kentucky, by Irvin Abell, MD 1926

A University is Born, by Margaret B. Ballard, MD, 1965, Garamond/Pridemark Press

Annals of Internal Medicine, 50th Anniversary Edition, American College of Physicians, July 1977

Bones, Molars and Briefs, The Yearbook of the University of Maryland

Bulletin Magazine, Medical Alumni Association of the University of Maryland, Inc., 1916-2006

Centennial Celebration of the Foundation of the University of Maryland, by John C. Hemmeter, 1908, Williams & Wilkins Company

Faculty Minutes, University of Maryland Baltimore Health Sciences and Human Services Library—Historical and Special Collections Department

Historical Sketch of the University of Maryland School of Medicine, by Eugene F. Cordell, MD, 1891, The Press of Isaac Friedenwald

Maryland Medical Journal, "Nathan Smith and the Johns Hopkins Connection," by Ronald H. Fishbein, MD, June 1989

Research and Discovery in Medicine, Contributions from Johns Hopkins, by A. McGehee Harvey, MD, 1981, The Johns Hopkins University Press

Some Account of the Rise and Progress of the University of Maryland, by Nathaniel Potter, MD, 1838, Joseph Robinson of Baltimore

Terra Mariae, The Yearbook of the University of Maryland

Terra Mariae Medicus, The Yearbook of the University of Maryland School of Medicine

The Dawn's Early Light, by Walter Lord, 1972, W. W. Norton & Co.

The Medical Annals of Maryland, by Eugene F. Cordell, MD, 1903, Williams & Wilkins Company

200 Years of Medicine in Baltimore, by Theodore E. Woodward, MD, 1976, Medical Alumni Association of the University of Maryland

Illustrative Credits

The vast majority of renderings, photographs, and medical artifacts displayed in this publication were drawn from the files of the Medical Alumni Association and the University of Maryland Baltimore Health Sciences and Human Services Library—Historical and Special Collections Department. Others are as noted below.

Pages 2–3,4–5,30–31,36–37,67
Renderings of Baltimore, courtesy of the Cator Collection, Enoch Pratt Free Library, Baltimore, Maryland

Pages 20,136
Watercolor Illustrations by Nancy Johnston

Pages 24,29,38,75,102
Sketches by artist Erin Dolan

Page 26
Rendering of John Wesley Davis, courtesy of the Architect of the Capitol, Collection of the U.S. House of Representatives

Page 65
James Carroll, courtesy of Mrs. Carolyn Carroll Buehler

Page 68
Photo of the Baltimore fire of 1904, courtesy of The Maryland Historical Society

Pages 68–69 & 116
Newspaper front pages, reprinted with the permission of the *Baltimore Sun*.

Page 79
Wounded soldier receiving emergency treatment on the front line—1918. Photo courtesy of the U.S. Army Military History Institute, Carlisle, Pennsylvania.

Page 86
Photograph of Henry Cotten, courtesy of New Jersey Archives, Department of State

For their contributions, the committee wishes to thank:
Frank M. Calia, MD, MACP
Ellen Beth Levitt, UMMS
Richard Lippenholz, Photographer
Andrew M. Malinow, MD, Class of 1981
Jessica Riescher, Photographer
Mark Teske, Photographer